To Sherie,

with a belief in
the future of marriage.

Mervin S. Field

The
Well-Seasoned
Marriage

THE WELL-SEASONED MARRIAGE

by Nina S. Fields, Ph.D.

Gardner Press, Inc.
NEW YORK & LONDON

GARDNER PRESS, INC.
19 Union Square West
New York, NY 10003

The author and publisher wish to thank the
copyright owners who have given their
permission to use copyrighted material.
Any ommissions or errors in giving proper
credit are unintentional and will be
corrected at the first opportunity after
the error or omission has been brought
to the attention of the author or publisher.

Library of Congress Cataloging-in-Publication Data
Fields, Nina S.
    The well-seasoned marriage.

    Bibliography: p.
    Includes index.
    1. Marriage—United States—Case studies. 2. Family
—United States—Case studies. 3. Communication in
marriage. I. Title.
HQ536.F54 1986   646.7'8   85-15880
ISBN 0-89876-114-X

Book design by Ray Solomon

To Maury,

with love

ACKNOWLEDGMENTS

During the course of writing this book I struggled continually to focus my ideas in ways that might be of interest to potential readers. While engaged in this project, I relied upon a number of people who played varied roles in moving the book along, I am pleased to acknowledge them now.

I am indebted to author Barbara Cohen for her belief in the value of this book, for her encouragement in getting it off the ground, and for her support and guidance through the final stages. Without her this book would never have been written. And I relish a side benefit that evolved as Barbara and I found increasing understanding of one another and a very special comradeship.

Special thanks to author Suzanne Lippset, who added organization and dimension to this book, and who found excitement in the concepts; and thanks to Marilyn Moorcroft for her careful editing.

My sincere appreciation to Dr. Joan Dasteel and Rheta Resnick for their critical reading of the first full draft, for alerting me to confusion in the text, and for suggesting ideas for my consideration. Kudos to my intrepid typist, Antonia Turman, a whiz at deciphering my illegible handwriting, and available at a moment's notice.

I am grateful to the California Institute for Clinical Social Work for its dissertation requirements that led to my study of long-term marriage and to the development of a disciplined approach to writing.

I am grateful to a warm circle of family and friends who encouraged me, and who provided a safe haven from the pressures of my three-year involvement in writing this book. Special thanks to Wendy Greene, Marilyn and Marvin Alkin, Marilynn and Richard Lieberman, Lorraine Meyer.

And I am grateful to two women in my life who profoundly influenced me—my loving mother, who gifted me with a joy in living and a belief in myself, and a loving grandmother who inspired a family. Warmest appreciation to our children who enrich the world and my life.

And most of all I am grateful to my husband, a most giving, loving man with whom I share the special rewards of a long-term marriage.

CONTENTS

Acknowledgments   *vii*

Introduction: The Study of Success   *3*

Chapter 1.
Together Yet Separate: With Equality for Each—the Key   *9*
Friendship With One's Mate   *10*
Friendships With Others   *11*
Separate Interests   *12*
Separateness and the Changing Times   *13*
    The Myth of "Incompleteness"   *16*
    The Burden of Dependency   *17*
    Work and Independence   *19*
The Trouble with Expectations   *21*
Exercises   *25*

Chapter 2.
Do You See Me Like I See Me?: The Route to Empathy   *27*
What It Is   *27*
Self-Knowledge: The First Step   *30*
    A Sense of Self: Being an Individual, Being a Mate *31*
    Things Inside Us   *32*
Common Blocks to Empathy   *33*
    Fears and Fantasies   *34*
    The Fear of Differences   *35*

Unexamined Parental Images and Imperfect Adult
     Sex Models   *36*
    Preconceptions and Expectations   *39*
Exercises   *40*

Chapter 3.
Money Is More than Dollars   *43*
Language of Money   *44*
When Bells Ring the Lights Come On   *48*
"Our" Money versus "My" Money   *50*
The Second Time Around   *51*
Money as Reward   *52*
Money as Control   *53*
Exercises   *57*

Chapter 4.
Sexuality: Keeping the Spark Alive   *61*
Ups and Downs in the Marriage Bed   *62*
What is Sexual Satisfaction?   *63*
    Trust   *64*
Openness and Communication   *67*
    Talking Straight   *68*
    Breaking Through Inhibitions   *69*
    Sexual Specifics   *71*
    Settling Old Grudges   *73*
    Affection   *75*
    Making Changes   *75*
The Whole View   *76*
Exercises   *77*

Chapter 5.
Marriage and Infidelity   *81*
The "Burden" of Monogamy   *81*
Agreeing in Principle   *84*
    Sex and Emotions   *85*
Lying   *89*
    Modern Marriages of Convenience   *89*
Stress: A Common Culprit   *91*

Agreed-on Adventures *93*
Midlife: Impact on Marriage *95*
    Some Like it Young *95*
    Change: Fun for Some, Hurtful for Others *96*
Conclusions *97*
Exercises *98*

Chapter 6.
Learning to Argue—the Right Way *99*
Shattering the Myths *100*
Argumentation as Communication *101*
    About Accommodation *104*
    Some Stoppers *105*
The Fear of Anger *106*
A Rogue's Gallery: How Not to Have an Argument *110*
    The Pulverizers *110*
    The Superior Being *111*
    The Freeze *112*
    The Clam and the Runaway *112*
    The Sneak Attacker *113*
Exercises *113*

Chapter 7.
Life with Children *117*
To Have or Have Not *118*
The Stresses to Expect *120*
    Jealousy and Resentment *120*
    Conflicts in Parenting Style *124*
    Special Alliances and Power Struggles *128*
    Living Through Children *128*
    Adolescence *130*
Life in the "Empty Nest" *132*
Exercises *136*

Chapter 8.
Parental Influence: Exorcising the Ghosts *139*
Who Turns You On—and Why *140*
Parental Models *143*

Separation: How to Accomplish It   *148*
   Impossible Parental Standards   *149*
   Meddling   *151*
Building Relations with In-laws   *154*
Caring for Parents in Need   *156*
Exercises   *159*

Epilogue   **163**

References   **165**

Bibliography   **167**

Index   **173**

The
Well-Seasoned
Marriage

INTRODUCTION
The Study of Success

"DIVORCE RATES SOAR!"
"Dramatic Increase in Single-Parent Families." "The Nuclear Family—A Thing of the Past!"

For more than a decade, the mass media have been ringing the death knell for marriage as an institution. Sociologists predict that one-third of marriages in the United States at any given moment will end in divorce. But ask yourself: If one-third are dissolved, does that not leave two-thirds intact? Two-thirds of the 75.1 million existing marriages is a pretty sizable number, not easily dismissed or ignored. This suggests that despite the changes our society has undergone in the last 20 or so years (the sexual revolution of the 1960s the resurgence of the women's movement, and the challenges to traditional family life growing out of the "permissive society" of the 1970s), millions of American adults are choosing marriage above all other options, new and old, as a way of life. For many of these people, being married to one mate with the expectation of staying married remains the best possible life-style in an imperfect world.

Neverless marriage as a way of life continues to get bad press. Countless popular books, articles, television programs, and movies concentrate on *failed* marriages and their aftermath. Scholarly and research efforts doggedly investigate the myriad reasons why marriages collapse. As a clinical social worker in private practice who has worked with families for

over 20 years, I too have focused much of my professional attention on troubled marriages and their repercussions. Over
the course of my career, I have observed and worked with
hundreds of married couples. Many of my patients did indeed
dissolve their marriages during the course of their therapy or
thereafter. For those people who had been married 20 or 25
years, it was a particularly jarring experience. But many chose
to remain in their marriages, often finding their relationships
clarified and revitalized in the process of psychotherapy. Personally I felt a growing interest, not in what makes marriages
fall apart, but in what makes them endure.

As my focus shifted from "failed" marriages to "successful"
ones, I began to sense that people in long-term marriages,
considered successful by both partners, often shared a kind of
experience not talked about in our society. In the midst of the
clamor over the traditional family's collapse, these people were
quietly living in a kind of intimacy rarely described or acknowledged, and were partaking in certain benefits far more
rewarding than most people realized. As a person involved in
a complex long-term marriage myself (this book will explore
the notion that all long-term marriages are complex), I
realized that my experience of marriage confirmed my intui-
tion: successful long-term marriages offer particular benefits—
special "perks" or rewards—that only the partners themselves
seem aware of and that even they rarely discuss.

I began tentatively to express my interest in long-term
marriages—marriages of more than 18 years' duration—and
in the characteristics they shared. Wherever I mentioned my
interest, I could be sure of evoking one particular response
among a variety of others: "Long-term marriage? You mean 20
years or so to the same person? Ugh."

Ugh? This response hardly applied to the successful relationships with which I was familiar.

It became clear that it was fashionable to disdain long-
term marital relationships, to turn up one's nose in favor of
other, less traditional life-styles.

But I still wondered about all those people who continue to
choose marriage and who put sincere effort into making it
work. Surely they could benefit from knowing that marriages
can and do last and that many people who remain married
for a considerable amount of time experience advantages in
their lives undreamed of by those just starting out. I decided
to study the phenomenon in earnest, and in 1979 developed

"A Study of Long-Term Successful Marriages."

The point of the study was to investigate a substantial number of relationships that met the criteria I specified for successful long-term marriages, and then to identify the features that they shared and that appeared to contribute to their success and stability. I felt I had a good chance of discovering a substantial number of marriages to meet my criteria in the middle and upper-middle-class population, where people have more time and energy to invest in a marital relationship than do those who are less economically advantaged.

Of the 1200 people who received them, nearly 300 husbands and wives who were married 18–30 years (145 couples) satisfactorily completed the questionnaires designed to elicit data on the factors shared by successful long-term marrieds. In the course of the study, I intensively interviewed 50 individuals from the sample, both individually and as couples, to gather more detailed and personalized (though still confidential) data to elucidate the questionnaire results.

My criterion for a long-term marriage was simple: the couple had to be married from 18 to 30 years. *The marriage was defined as successful if both partners completed three key items interspersed in the questionnaire with either "all of the time" or "most of the time."* These items were: (1) I love my mate; (2) I feel I married the best mate for me; and (3) I wish to remain in this marriage. The questionnaires themselves revealed whether both did indeed view their marriage in this light, and of the the 290 subjects included in the study, three-quarters turned out to meet the "success" criteria. The respondents were not aware of the intent of the study, or that their "success" was being measured.

This book, then, is based on the results of the 1979 study (referred to in this book as the California study), on my experience in clinical practice, and on a thorough reading of the professional literature on marriage. It is written explicitly for those Americans who are getting and staying married, choosing the emotional security and commitment to permanence that are the hallmark of the successful long-term marital relationship.

It has insights for couples newly married, for long-term marrieds, for couples who are experiencing difficulties, and for those who just want to make their marriages better. Such couples have much to learn from others who have lived rich lives together over many years. This book offers an array of techniques to open channels of understanding and communication designed to enhance intimacy and overall marital satisfaction.

Each chapter explores a single factor found to be essential to the development of a satisfying long-term marital relationship: overall sexual satisfaction, each partner's sense of individual identity and an egalitarian partnership, an ability to view the other as he or she sees himself or herself (which leads to empathy), a commitment to marriage, a talent for and willingness to resolve conflict, and efforts to relate to parents and children in a reasonable way.

This book is filled with quotations from the interviews and from my private-practice files. Some of the longer extracts are dramatizations based on interviews with more than one person or on material that was provocative but too sketchy in the original. These stories convey the essence of the healthy long-term marriage by supplying details both of conflicts and mistakes and of those benefits that I long suspected to be characteristic of long-term marriages and that motivated my study. Often both sorts of details appear at first to be too trivial to warrant attention. But from a patient I long ago learned that in marriage "trivial" is not necessarily synonymous with "unimportant." This woman could not bear the way her husband clicked his fork against his teeth when he ate.

"That seems like a pretty minor complaint," I remarked.

She shot me a withering glance, still bristling with irritation at the memory of her husband's eating habits. "Little things," she said, "are unimportant only on the surface."

For this woman all she disliked in her husband was symbolized by the click of his fork. In another seemingly "little thing," described by a husband of 28 years, I was given a glimpse of one of the benefits he had been deriving from his marriage for more than a quarter of a century—a small detail that summed up the satisfaction he took in his marriage:

> Ever since I met her she's sung a single line of a certain song for a month or so, then gone on to a different line—only one—from a different song. Never sings the whole song, just one line. I used to suspect it was a momentary hint of the music going on inside her all the time. By now, after 28 years,

I *know* that's what it is. Inside she's just singing away, and she has been for as long as I've known her. It's great, knowing that about the person you live with, don't you think?

This book invites you to find the song inside of you.

1

TOGETHER YET SEPARATE
With Equality for Each—the Key

THROUGHOUT THIS BOOK I will identify various elements as prerequisites to a healthy, enduring marriage: empathy, open communication, trust, sexual satisfaction, and a view of your mate that matches your mate's picture of himself or herself. Look closely at this list and you will realize that all five factors imply a reaching out between two separate people. Seems obvious? Not worth mentioning? Not so. Success in marriage, as the California study and many others confirm, depends primarily on the partners' maintenance of their separate identities while simultaneously reaching out to each other to create a life together. This is the lesson behind all the chapters in this book: success in marriage rests on the seemingly contradictory combination of separateness and togetherness.

Separate yet together—what does it mean? It simply means that in the prototype of the successful marriage two complete individuals come together voluntarily to form a loving relationship that endures over time. These marriage partners know they are whole people when they are apart, have a strong sense of themselves as individuals with distinct attitudes, interests, and desires, and feel able to participate in life alone. Simultaneously they consciously relish the time they spend with their mates and choose to share their lives with them. Interestingly, the subjects of the study discussed a range of specific techniques that helped them to maintain this balance between individuality and life as a couple. We will explore some of the more frequently cited techniques.

FRIENDSHIP WITH ONE'S MATE

Many study subjects mentioned the friendship they experience with their mates as the factor most responsible for the success of their marriages. By this they meant a camaraderie that underlay all the other, sometimes more complex aspects of their relationships, such as their parenting responsibilities, their sex lives, and their financial and householding activities. Friendship, this more fundamental aspect of their relationship, seemed to be a confirmation of the "otherness" of each partner and of the pleasure each mate took in spending time with the other. This quality was the very antithesis of the kind of unhealthy dependency that mates can develop on one another when they are insecure about themselves as valuable individuals or about their rightful places in the world. Rather the friendliness these partners feel for each other represented their clear choice—not need—to be together, a choice that they made actively throughout their marriages.

Matthew gives a good account of the special quality of friendship that characterizes his marriage with Adele

> We were always good friends, long before we even thought about getting married. We always went places together or just hung around together, it seemed so natural. At some point we began to have a sexual relationship, too, and that's when we thought about getting married. When we finally did, we carried our friendship over into the marriage and the result has been a kind of contentment I think is very special. Most of the time we just feel relaxed with one another—though we had a lot to learn and a lot to work out, I admit. We just usually felt companionable and comfortable, and able somehow to reach each other.

Laura and Arnold, married 18 years, are both small–plane enthusiasts who originally met in a flying club. Says Laura:

> We always had flying in common and still do, and both of us

have great fun with it. The whole flying scene is tremendously social, and I still get as excited looking forward to a club event as I did years ago. But the best part has been sharing it with Arn. It's funny, we can have troubles galore—with the kids, the house, the financial situation—and really build up some irritations with each other and then go off on a flying weekend and all the tension disappears; we just have fun, as always. I've always felt that feeling, that ability to enjoy each other, is the core of our marriage and the secret of our success. I look around and see my friends' marriages and some of them don't have much fun together at all. We're really lucky on that score, I think.

FRIENDSHIPS WITH OTHERS ·

"A friend is someone who likes you," says a charming children's book, and indeed people need others in their lives to "like them." Friendships enrich peoples' lives by adding a variety of personalities, of interests, of talents to spark their world. They allow for emotional intimacy and the building of deep relationships that are valuable in good times and bad times. You can rely on a world larger than you and your mate; you can share that world while still maintaining a special relationship with your husband or wife.

Men and women blossom when they do not feel confined to associating only with people who are approved of by their mates. There is room both for joint friendships and for separate ones (when a mate is not interested in the association). Couple activities are fun, but so is a lunch date with an old friend.

The question of how free you are to maintain friendships with the opposite sex probably harkens back to how trusting you are in your marital relationship. Can men and women go to lunch, dinner, a hockey game, or the ballet with an opposite-sex colleague or friend? Why not? If no ulterior motive exists, you should feel free. If your mate wants to join you, he or she should be included. If the reason for joining you is not out of genuine interest but out of fear, then you should both talk about the mistrust. Generally speaking men and women stay on the safest ground when their separate pals are of their own sex.

SEPARATE INTERESTS

Taking pleasure in each other as friends in no way precludes having separate interests. In a way the fact that each partner in a marriage has a distinct set of interests confirms that each is indeed expressing and exercising a separate identity, a distinct sense of self, apart from the "coupledom" of marriage. Compare the following two excerpts, and guess which woman is involved in a successful long-term marriage and which is in dire need of building her self-esteem.

> Roger is a very vibrant, very smart person. I've always felt if I just stuck with him I'd learn a lot, and that's about what I've done since we got married. I hang around in the background and listen—all the wives do. We're all married to professors who have been on the same faculty for years, and that's been our social life in total for about the last six years. Oh, the women like each other, but the men are the real inner circle— sometimes I feel as though we make dinner so the guys can get together and pontificate. The circle of people is very active, but maybe that's not the greatest thing. I haven't done anything else, seen anyone else in the lord knows how long; I feel as though I'm playing the role that Roger prescribed for me, and maybe not even that well. Still he's the smartest man I've ever met and I've learned so much in these years I would never have known without him.

Now, here is Hilary's account of how her growing interest in photography affected her marriage to Jim.

> I took pictures all through college and fooled around in the darkroom. In our first year of marriage, we had a party and an agent came. He loved my pictures and asked if he could buy two of them; suddenly I'd turned professional! Those first sales did so much for me—I just wanted to get better and better all the time, and I really worked at it. It was the perfect kind of work, too, because I could do it while the children were growing up—go into the darkroom after dinner, in the morning before anyone woke up, that sort of thing. Jim's architectural work too was somewhat adaptable, especially since he has his office and studio at home. I think my favorite all-time feeling, and the one on which our marriage is based, is the one that comes when the kids are all busy and I'm in the darkroom while Jim's in his office—an awareness that we're both working in different parts of the house, feeling secure about each other's presence but just moving along on our own projects. Jim would agree, I think. He loves his work and loves knowing that I love mine. Too many women feel left out, I think, be-

cause they have nothing to match their husbands' work. And too many men reinforce that feeling by interfering with their wives' pursuit of separate interests—perhaps they want to keep their wives' attention focused on themselves. Or is that changing now? Maybe I'm still in the Dark Ages – spending too much time in the darkroom thinking about the pictures I take.

Having emphasized the importance of separate interests, it is worthwhile to stress that shared interests, too, can enrich the relationship between marriage partners. Couples who share interests and leisure activities—like Laura and Arnold, the fliers described earlier—obviously spend more time together and come to know each other more fully than those who retain a wholly private pocket of life cut off from the marriage. And a not unimportant fact is that such couples can have a lot of fun together. Almost all the respondents in our study mentioned having fun with their mates a good part of the time. It helps to be able to laugh together, to lighten up when life gets bumpy, to look for the humor in otherwise difficult situations. That sense of humor can go a long way in accepting each others' foibles. Marriage works for those who work *and* play at it.

SEPARATENESS AND THE CHANGING TIMES

The subjects of the California study have lived through a major transition period in our society. They grew up in the 1940s and '50s, when sex roles were perhaps as rigid as any time in history: women were either spinsters or wives, mothers, and homemakers; men were bachelors or husbands, fathers, and breadwinners. Each of those roles, as we know, had its proscribed behaviors, and the media strenuously reinforced them all. Thus men rarely changed diapers, washed dishes, or stayed home with the kids without being considered eccentric, and even suspiciously "effeminate." Women rarely went out socially on their own or went to work for any but the direst financial reasons, and then at the risk of shaming the man by openly calling into question his role. Grown women asked their husband's permission to do what they wanted to do, and both women and men took it for granted that the man in the family had the last word on household matters. That is just the way things were.

But in the 1960s the traditional family structure began to be shaken, and the late '60s brought the revival of the feminism that had been waxing and waning in this country for almost a century. An analysis of why sex roles started to grow more flexible is outside the scope of this book, but that they did so is very much to the point. All the subjects of the California study were married by the mid-1960s, and they all brought to their marriages the traditional roles they had learned as they grew up. Within that context togetherness was valued, but separateness, the second component of our formula for a successful long-term marriage, was viewed with suspicion. Thus these people had to experiment and work on their own, without much encouragement from society, to evolve the together-yet-separate balance that we have identified as a key to the success of a long-term marriage.

It must be said, however, that the hard work necessary to implement this formula is not limited to people of the 1950s generation. Old patterns die hard, and many who wholeheartedly approve of the new, more egalitarian sex roles have difficulty incorporating them into their own day-to-day lives. Ideally our ideas and feelings mesh in a way that gives us comfort, but in real life we frequently find a distance between our thoughts and feelings, a distance that can cause emotional and mental distress.

Toby and Stan are examples of people in a relationship in which the split between ideas and feelings regarding egalitarian sex roles in marriage is easy to see. Toby had a fairly well-developed sense of herself when she met Stanley. She had done very well in college, where she majored in business, and was generally considered to have a sparkling career ahead of her. At the age of 22, she felt she could tackle just about anything, and she took a job with a well-known department store as a buyer's assistant. She had a flair for fashion and was assertive enough about her own ideas to feel confident with, not intimidated by, her bosses. At about the time Toby was learning the ropes in her job, she met Stan, just out of law school and intensely involved in building his fledgling practice. Thus both Toby and Stan were spending much of their energy to build their professional careers, while grabbing some moments to be together. They both understood the demands of their respective careers and, far from begrudging each other the time they spent independently, felt lucky to have found prospective mates who were so understanding and who felt no jealousy or resentment about the separate aspect of their lives.

When Stan and Toby married, however, things changed, as Stan very candidly reported in an early therapy session.

> I don't know why, but once we were married my feelings changed. I began to feel resentful of the outside demands on Toby that interfered with our time together at home, and I felt that if she really loved me, she would rather be at home than off doing things for her work. Deep inside I felt it was okay for me to be busy with my law practice, but I began to grouch at her if her outside life didn't mesh with mine. You know, I always thought of myself as a very understanding man who believed in equality for women, but my insides got all tangled up about it in my own marriage, I mouthed the words about independent women, but I couldn't stand to see my wife be truly independent.
>
> What happened to me? I'm still not sure. How come I was attracted to an independent woman and liked Toby's self-reliant style while we were dating but got so screwed up after we were married? I think maybe the word "marriage" limited us, as though it was no longer okay to be the carefree people we had been. I think I took on the attitude that I thought society expected of me. Now I want to challenge the traditional rules, and I'm ready to work on my feelings in therapy.

The story is not unusual, except perhaps in Stan's acceptance of his need for professional help. When men and women are forging new ways of relating to each other, they are bound to get caught up in old notions along the way. Some of Stan's feelings about a woman's availability to her husband and a man's "rights" to his wife's time had their origin in his traditional upbringing, where these tenets went unchallenged. Though intellectually Stan had rejected his parents' kind of marriage, inside him persisted the effects of growing up in that very home. Formalizing his relationship with Toby in marriage apparently triggered an unconscious analogy in Stan between his parents' marriage as a model and his own, as yet undeveloped and unformed. This pattern is not unfamiliar, nor is the one in which a thought–feeling discrepancy arises when children come. (We will see that child rearing taps our deepest insecurities.) Where we suddenly feel uncertain about how to proceed, is it any wonder that the ways we learned as children come into play? Where these old feelings conflict with new beliefs, it takes hard work, sometimes guided by a therapist, first to understand the situation, then to work through the feelings, and gradually to reconcile ideas and emotions.

The Myth of "Incompleteness"

Men are not the only ones who experience thought–feeling discrepancies with respect to the new separate-and-equal sex roles that have emerged over the past two decades. Women often strongly support the ideology of female independence while experiencing great difficulty incorporating their ideas into their private lives. Consider Alison's comment on her ability to feel separate from her husband:

> I always thought I would do fine on my own but it still scared me to feel I could be happy alone for a whole day, a whole week, without any great need to see Todd. Shouldn't I miss him? Is what I feel really a deep love if I feel so good doing things with other people and am happy that I can do what I want without him? I love being with Todd but I love my separate life too, and it makes me wonder whether I really love him enough to be married to him.

Alison fears her strength, seeing it as limiting the depth of her feeling for Todd, but in reality she is giving in to what I call the myth of incompleteness. This is a vestige of the fantasy that underlies much of what some people call love. Movies, stories, and especially popular songs highlight such sentiments as "I'll die if I can't be with you," "My life will end if you leave me," and "I only feel real when we're together." The underlying idea is that the more incomplete you are without the loved one, the greater, the more profound, is your love for that person. Taken to its logical conclusion, this position can only engender a manufactured dependency, probably salted by a subliminal resentment at the need to squelch one's feelings of independence for the sake of maintaining the feeling of love. Thus we find many women who radiate strength and freedom in the world at large but who surprise themselves and others with their need to be weak and dependent within marriage or other intimate relationships. The book *The Cinderella Complex* deals precisely with this important issue that inhibits independence in women. In truth, as the California study demonstrates clearly, the most long-lived love relationships occur between two people who feel great when with their loved ones but who know they could survive without them, who consider their relationships to have enlarged their experience and enriched their lives, but who also look for fulfillment within themselves. Such people, whose marriages epitomize the separateness/togetherness balance, would clearly feel bereft at the loss of the loved one, but would have the reserves to continue on alone.

The Burden of Dependency

The myth of incompleteness applies to men as well as women, and so does its corollary, the burden of dependency, which can be felt by the other partner in an unequal relationship. The story of Dana and his wife Margaret exemplifies this pattern more clearly than would a lengthy description.

From the beginning of their marriage, Dana felt good about making all the major decisions for Margaret and himself—regarding the house they bought, for instance, the kind of car they drove, and so on. Dana trusted Margaret not to challenge his decisions and felt proud of her complete reliance on him. Once their two children were born, the decisions that were necessary seemed to multiply out of hand, though, and Dana started thinking it might be nice if Margaret took some of the decision making on herself. Unfortunately Margaret had learned the habit of dependency too well. She believed in Dana's superiority and that her deference to him in all matters proved how much she loved him. But after seven years of marriage, Dana's attraction to his wife's dependent "femininity" had turned sour. He resented the time it took to advise her and began to consider her not charmingly passive and yielding, but downright incompetent and unworthy of respect. He felt as if he had three children, not two, and long after he realized that he sincerely wanted a divorce he remained married, though dissatisfied and distraught, for fear that Margaret would be unable to get along without him. It took him several years to grow exasperated enough to leave Margaret, despite his reservations.

In contrast, here is a couple who grew out of the old ways into a new style of living together that was satisfactory to them both. Ellen was raised in a small midwestern city by parents who had very little experience of the world. She expected to marry a man who would take care of her—the proper function of the man in a marriage according to her parents, and her as well. She never seriously considered pursuing a career or earning her own living. Rather she readied herself for the role for which she felt destined: that of a wife and mother under the protection and guidance of her husband. After high school Ellen got a job in a local department store and attended college part-time, taking a liberal arts course. She met Don when he was a senior in college and she stopped going to school when they married. During the early years, she looked up to her husband's superior knowledge, accepted him as the main decision maker, and was very dependent upon him. She felt he was much smarter than she was and that his decisions were almost always the right ones, so she considered her dependence on him to be "sensible." However, as the years passed, she grew to have a greater appreciation of her own knowledge, through participation in community activities and taking courses at the local college.

By the 12th year of the marriage, she was able to question her husband's judgment more frequently. She risked offering solutions to family problems, and expressed some of her own opinions in many areas. She felt that her husband encouraged this growth, though it meant that they needed to discuss many more things than they had previously, and at greater length.

When her youngest child was 15, Ellen began to pursue a career as a buyer for a prestigious department store, a job with exciting growth potential. In this she was spurred on by the changes in the society around her and by similar moves she saw some of her married friends begin to make. Gradually, as she was called upon to use her skills, she developed more confidence in herself, emerging as a full-grown woman whose competencies were valued. Within the family she saw with pleasure that she had changed from a passive-dependent child/woman into a well functioning adult woman. Don admired the change and encouraged her emergence. Sometimes he wondered if it might not be nice to have Ellen in a subservient position again, but soon recognized how much he enjoyed the sharing of the load, rather than taking sole responsibility for their lives.

At 42, then, Ellen had fully emerged as an equal partner

in marriage despite her traditional upbringing. Similarly Don, who had a demanding business, was relieved of the sole responsibility for the family's well-being and delighted in his wife's growing role as a dependable ally, breadwinner and stimulating companion. His need to be the "authority, provider" changed as his wife outgrew her socially conditioned need to have a "daddy" in her life. Thus these two achieved the mutual respect and mutual sharing cited by many in the California study as major conditions for satisfaction in marriage.

Work and Independence

The task of achieving a balance between togetherness and separateness does not end when a woman gets a job. In many ways the real work of remolding sex roles and breaking down expectations begins only then, since feelings often conflict with ideals when it comes to dividing up the household responsibilities in nontraditional ways.

Susan and Eric were satisfied in the early years of their marriage to focus on Eric's professional needs as a physician. Eric's medical practice took time to build and Susan was content to be available to Eric, entertaining their friends and running the household around his schedule. Susan also became active in her local community, rising to important positions with the PTA and League of Women Voters. As much as she enjoyed her children and her family life, she took enormous satisfaction in her outside activities, and at a certain point decided to pursue some of her personal interests more seriously. The children were all in school and there was much more time available to her. She soon began to realize, however, that her family encouraged her to pursue her own interests only as long as she was as available to them as ever and had plenty of time to fulfill all her household responsibilities. It was great for wife and mom to become her own person just as long as the house still ran smoothly and no extra demands were placed on anyone else.

Susan struggled with feelings that she was being "selfish" and with a sense of guilt for "abandoning" the family that needed her. On the other hand, she knew that Eric and the children were perfectly capable of taking care of themselves, and that in any case they could afford a weekly house cleaner to keep things in order, especially if Susan were bringing in a second income. Finally she decided that though women are biologically destined to bear children, there is no reason that their entire lives should be limited to a housekeeping function. She began to ask Eric to plan to take on some of the car-pooling and other duties that she had always performed. She suggested that all family members take turns at cooking, shopping, and doing the wash while she did some intensive job seeking. The oppressive feeling that she had to be responsible for all parts of their domestic lives began to lift.

Susan has just begun coping with the reactions of her husband and children to the major changes her new job has effected in their lives. The full impact will take some time to reveal itself. However, Eric has mellowed. He is more understanding than he was earlier in the marriage and now acknowledges Susan's needs to exercise her own potential—not to mention that Susan's success in the future could ease the financial burden on him considerably. "Maybe it's worth it to stop thinking that the old way, where everyone knew what was expected from a man or woman was the best and only way. I'm game, and it's beginning to make more and more sense to me, though sometimes it feels like a lot of complication has been added to my life. Car-pooling on my afternoon off is not quite what I had in mind for my free time."

For a majority of women, the choice of whether or not to work is not theirs: financial concerns force them to join the work force. To some men the fact that they earn the living makes them feel that they have already done their share for the family, and they see no reason to do more when they get home. Other men recognize that running a household is a major undertaking and that it complements the man's contribution through his job. But where husband and wife are both working, it makes sense to agree that just as the work outside is divided between the married partners, so the running of the home must be split—and not along preconceived, role-determined lines. Thus the partner who likes to cook could cook more often; the one with a sense of order might straighten the house. If one has a major preference, of course it should be honored where possible, but nobody should end up with all of the undesirable jobs. The important thing is to value each other, accommodate each other, and arrive at solutions that feel right to both. Here again the creation of an appropriate life–style together becomes the first priority and it is a process that is bound to require much talk, much compromise, and probably a substantial amount of time. Yet, as we have seen, it is just such an extended dialogue and such a mutual investment of energy that proves the committment of both partners to continuing and strengthening the relationship. In this way the hard work of creating and sustaining a long-term marriage that meets both partners' needs becomes its own reward.

THE TROUBLE WITH EXPECTATIONS

A final word is in order on changing sex roles and the creation of more egalitarian marriages than were encouraged in the past. It has to do with the power of expectations and the need some of us have at times to realize we are being impeded by our own fantasy images of the way things should be. Just as our parental models can influence our lives heavily without our even realizing that they are important to us at all, so old ideas, often formed before we have had enough practical experience to know that an infinite number of ways of life is possible, can limit our imagination. These old ideas can keep us on a conventional track when innovation and experimentation may be the means of our fulfillment.

Deborah, for instance, married to Frank for 20 years, expresses the disappointment she felt with real life after she had immersed herself in romances and movie magazines in her youth and had planned her own marriage accordingly.

> The "Hollywood marrriage" really stayed with me. I expected to be dashing off to big parties and Riviera-type vacations all the time and to be swooning with sexual excitement constantly. I fed off pop magazines and really bought it all. I thought Elizabeth Taylor was the luckiest person in the world because she was so beautiful, and I really worked hard to be beautiful—and still do, though it gets harder. All in all I expected life with Frank to be like a movie. You can imagine how I felt being bogged down by diapers and money worries. I felt disappointed for a long time after I got married, and I still wish life could be like it seemed for Elizabeth, though I have finally learned it can't.

Deborah's head was cluttered with fantasy—not a bad thing in itself, but in this case the fantasy stood between her and the true potential for her marriage. Her fantasy was too

impractical to be realized. Conversely fantasy can be a prelude
to change where it represents an active imagining of the way
things *could*, not *should* be—that is, where the fantasizer pro-
jects possibilities as part of an effort to effect a change.

Jane and Jerrold both had traditional expectations about
what married life should be like. They grew up in the 1940s
and 50s, married in the early 1960s, and set up a household
that conformed wholly to their parents' model. They lived in
an expensive suburb, split the responsibilities along conventional lines, with Jerrold as breadwinner and Jane as
homemaker, and settled down to a pleasant existence that
both, looking back, admitted was humdrum. In their third
year of marriage, when their first daughter was a year old,
Jane gave birth to a child with Down's syndrome, and their
whole life came crashing down. Nothing could have been
farther from their expectations of what their lives would be
like. Thus not only did they have the child's condition to adjust to, but they had to cope with the crumbling of their
routine as well. What would happen now that they no longer
had the comfort of knowing that the traditional ways would
carry them safely into old age? What could they depend on?
What was life supposed to be like now?

It took a long time, more than two years, for Jerrold and
Jane to absorb the reality of having a disabled child and to
rid themselves of their old expectations of how their lives
would go. But then Jane started doing some very productive
fantasizing, imagining ways to combat what she considered
the most difficult aspect of their new life—isolation. Both she
and Jerrold felt cut off from their old friends by the enormity
of their baby's condition and its effects on the family. Jane's
imagination led her to wonder how she could reach other
families with the same problem and what they might do to
help each other. Ultimately she conceived of a support group
that would meet on a regular basis and share experiences as
well as information on community resources and education
possibilities for children with Down's syndrome. Though Jane
had always considered herself very retiring and wholly without
interest or talent in community affairs, she struggled with her
shyness to make the first move, and soon had placed ads in
local papers, had contacted public service agencies, and had
even made a public service announcement on a local television
station. Soon afterward the group she had imagined was in
existence, and within a year it was in contact with other such

groups nationwide. Jane slowly found that she had a career for herself as a public speaker and information processor as she became more deeply involved in creating a formal network linking the local groups across the nation and in developing a national newsletter.

Jerrold had been enthusiastic about Jane's involvement from the start, and had profited greatly from his involvement in the support group. But when she began to be drawn into her new role as organizer and administrator for the national network, his own conventions bristled. He had never seen himself as the type of man to be married to a career woman, and had hardly expected to be challenged on this point. He assumed the old-school point of view that a man with a working wife was somehow inadequate to the task of providing for his family. Jane felt a sense of involvement and satisfaction too strong to sacrifice, and she overcame her own respect for convention to insist on her right to follow her conscience and to do the work she chose—or that had chosen her, for she did feel destined to follow her vocation. There followed some very turbulent years for Jerrold and Jane as they struggled to rid themselves of the old stereotypes and to find a way to live together under the new conditions in their lives. They did manage to create a new kind of family for themselves, but the first step was to exorcise the demon expectations they had brought to their marriage so they could free their imaginations to come up with new possibilities. The results of their testing those possibilities in a trial-and-error way was a marriage bond strengthened by their mutual effort, and pride in each other for transcending their old traditional, inhibiting ways. Only after their affection, trust, and desire to stay together carried them through some very difficult times did Jerrold and Jane become a model of the separateness/togetherness balance.

One final story exemplifies some of the impact when roles are reversed as a result of circumstance.

Frances, a tall, red-haired woman with sparkling green eyes, was shy and ill at ease with strangers when she met Tony, an outgoing, blunt man who communicated in a rough manner, except where his wife was concerned. With Frances he was patient, considerate of her feelings, and uncritical. He was very much in love with her and took pride in both his family and his consulting firm. After 18 years of marriage, Frances decided to expand her world from the role of wife and mother and took a job on a part-time basis in a center for abused children. As she described it:

> I felt as though I knew nothing about the outside world. So many years had been devoted to the family, and of course I was so shy that it took all my courage to approach getting a job. Tony encouraged me. I grew, oh, did I grow. I learned so much about the importance of communicating my needs, my feelings, and gradually I stopped being so dependent, so shy, so sensitive. A new world opened up to me with our children and with our friends. I could respect myself because I felt appreciated in a world away from my family. What a shock when Tony had a heart attack and I, who had only done part-time work for five years, was thrown suddenly into being the full-blown breadwinner. I was scared to death, but somehow managed. It was awful at first for Tony. He felt so guilty about depriving us all. He and I suddenly reversed roles, and it took time for us to become accustomed to a life where he did the cooking and some of the household routines while I got myself a full-time job so we'd have an income for us to live on. Our kids have been out of the house for the past two years, so the money problems have not been so bad. It's taken time for us fully to adjust to this new life, and it also took a therapist's help to deal with the fright of the heart attack. But now Tony and I laugh and wonder why it took a heart attack for us to look at our life-style and change. Where is it written that women have to cook? Tony loves to cook and he's much more creative in that area than I. We learned to be flexible in our life together.

Tony and Frances grew up with ideas of a very traditional family with the man as the dominant breadwinner, and the woman as the dependent child-rearer and housewife. Their lifestyle was based on whatever economic level the man could achieve. Her timidity fit like a glove to his more assured demeanor. However, even without her husband's heart attack, Frances had wanted to be more than she was and had already begun making efforts to change. She and her husband had shared a warm relationship, and Tony did not feel threatened when Frances began to meet interesting men or became expert in a field about which he knew little. Their relationship became much more equal in all respects. Tony was obviously ready for more equality, but the role reversal came as a blow to him, one that he and Frances took time to reconcile.

To grow together, to enjoy being dominant in some areas and dependent in others, to feel that you may sometimes be the rudder, at other times the wheel, all that helps people to enjoy their long-term relationship.

A character in Chaucer's *Canterbury Tales* (1396) stated the case for equality in this way:

For, gentlemen, there is one thing I may safely assert: lovers who wish to live together for any length of time must submit to one another. Love will not be constrained by mastery: when mastery appears, then the God of Love flaps his wings, and presto! he's gone! Love is a thing as free as any spirit. Women by their nature desire liberty, not to be constrained like bondslaves; and if I'm not mistaken, so do men.

EXERCISES

The following exercises are designed to help you examine some of your feelings and attitudes.

1. You and your mate should answer the questions without consulting each other. When finished, compare your answers and discuss the similarities and differences. Listen to understand what your mate feels.

1 = most of the time

2 = some of the time

3 = rarely or never

	Most	Some	Rarely
I feel we are equals.	1	2	3
I enjoy separate activities.	1	2	3
I feel upset by my mate's hobbies.	1	2	3
I wish I had more time to pursue my own interests.	1	2	3
I wish my mate had more separate interests.	1	2	3
I feel my mate is my friend.	1	2	3
I like to participate in activities with my mate.	1	2	3
I feel my mate is too dependent on me.	1	2	3
I resent my mate's work.	1	2	3
Our life together pleases me.	1	2	3
I feel there are too many demands on my time.	1	2	3

	Most	Some	Rarely
My mate's independence frightens me.	1	2	3
I like traditional roles.	1	2	3
It would be nice to make some changes in the way we run our home.	1	2	3
I feel I do more than my share in our life together.	1	2	3
I feel disappointed by our life.	1	2	3
I feel my mate and I have enough time together.	1	2	3
I feel my mate understands me.	1	2	3
I feel my mate tries to make me happy.	1	2	3
I feel my mate is overly critical of me.	1	2	3
I feel I don't know how to please my mate.	1	2	3
I feel my mate doesn't know how to please me.	1	2	3
I feel my mate respects me.	1	2	3
I feel my mate wants me to change.	1	2	3
I feel my mate likes me.	1	2	3

Now compare your responses with those of your mate and talk together. Try to understand how the other feels.

2. If the first exercises revealed dissatisfaction in any area, select one thing you would like to change and discuss it with your mate.

3. If you feel your independence is not allowed enough room, talk about what you would like. If, on the other hand, you feel too dependent, see if you and your mate can take some action to change it, for example, for a social outing, or taking over the checkbook.

4. Sometimes awareness does not lead to change. If you find yourself in that position, consider getting professional help.

2

DO YOU SEE ME LIKE I SEE ME?

The Route to Empathy

WHAT IT IS

Empathy—WE HEAR THE word a lot in a time like ours when there's so much talk about feelings. But what does it really mean? Why is this quality important in our interpersonal relations? And why is it often difficult to achieve, especially in our family life, where it counts the most?

Quite simply, as we all know, to empathize is to "feel for" another. We gain this ability when we are able to let go of our own needs and feelings in order to put ourselves in another's shoes. In marriage we extend the idea not only to seeing the world as the other views it, but also to seeing the person as that individual sees himself or herself. People who can perceive others in this way are apt to be more in tune with their mates and thus have a greater capacity for empathy than those focused permanently on their own view of others in their lives.

Stretch your imagination. What kind of a man is your husband, completely apart from yourself? How does he experience himself—all the time, not just at home after a hard day, but when he is out to breakfast with the men, at work in a tense meeting, with the kids when you are not there? What

are his satisfactions, his frustrations, the worries and pleasures he carries with him? What shakes his confidence? What
does he hope to accomplish in his life? What are the qualities
about him that give him pride?

What kind of a woman, alone and apart from you is your
wife? How does she perceive herself as she goes through the
day—at work with her boss? at lunch with her friends? all
alone after the kids are in bed? What thoughts does she
think? What pleases her, aggravates her, gives her satisfaction? What is her idea of work well done? What does she expect from her life over the long run?

The ability to answer such questions accurately reflects a
capacity for empathy. The California study showed empathy to
be strongly related to satisfaction in marriage. Stated another
way, in the long-term marriages deemed successful by the
criteria of the study, the partners showed a marked ability to
perceive their mates as their mates perceived themselves.
Some of the participants (the women more frequently than
the men) tended to view their mates more positively than the
mates viewed themselves, but as long as their images of their
mates were rooted in reality, these idealizations appeared to
have a positive effect on the relationship.

Let us look at a rather traditional couple whose ability to
view each other realistically comes through loud and clear in
their descriptions of each other. Meet Gil and Elaine, married
for 22 years and the parents of three teenaged girls.

GIL: I think of myself as a warm, loving man, family cen-
tered and secure in my marriage. At work I'm aggressive when I
have to be, tough-talking more than I like to be, and ambitious
for my sake and for my wife and kids. Maybe I don't express
my tender feelings much, but I have them. Often when I come
home at night, I'm so worn out I'm a bundle of nerves. All I see
is that the kids have left their bedroom lights on or the car
wasn't put away, and I start crabbing about that. I just forget
to say I'm glad I'm home and happy to see everybody, even
though I've been thinking about them with pleasure on my way
home.

ELAINE: It used to really get to me—Gil would come home
and he'd start to criticize us and pick on us as soon as he
walked in the door. I'd get mad and start to match him complaint for complaint. After all, when the children were babies,
we both had a lot to complain about. But as the years went on,
things got easier: I started to *hear* what he said about work
and to appreciate the stress he was under. When he'd start get-

ting to me, I'd stop him and say, "Hey wait a minute. What happened today?" trying to find out what was *really* bothering him, thinking about what it must be like to work for his insensitive boss, or spending time with his colleagues, who I knew were a very competitive bunch. I began to realize how much it meant to him to do a good job and how he felt about himself when things went wrong—and why he cared. It was because of us, sure, but also because of his need to do anything he did well. After all that need to do good work was part of what made me love him in the first place, when we were first in college together. Now I know he loves us and thinks of us, but that his work matters to him too, and that he's right to be upset if things go wrong.

As for me, I've always cared about running a safe, clean, beautiful house. Nobody thinks much of running a house as work these days, but I was raised to take pride in a well-run house, and I do. When Gil used to come home and criticize things, I felt he was like all the rest of them—he didn't think I did much at all; he thought caring for three babies, keeping the house up, shopping, cooking, doing volunteer work, driving people around was what I did to fill time until he came home. But slowly, as we worked things out, I started feeling as if he appreciated my work more, that he'd stopped to think about it and actually understand what I do and that I take pride in *my* work too.

GIL: In those early years, I was really caught up in my career and didn't think much about how Elaine spent her time. I mean, she did what a wife was supposed to do, right? I remember one day casually looking over this calendar she kept on the wall by the phone. "Good Lord," I thought. Every morning, every afternoon, every weekend moment was blocked out with appointments, meetings, places to take the kids to. It looked just like my calendar at work—but I only had two people under me and no responsibility for running the office. She had the three kids under her, plus me to schedule for and to be with, plus the house to run, and her own interests to pursue—she was involved in town politics then. I was impressed. I remember looking at the kids and the house in a new way, thinking she's really great at keeping things in shape and getting things done. I started telling her I thought she was doing a terrific job! And I remember seeing a look in her eye, half-amused, half-exasperated, that meant, "It's about time you noticed, you bum!"

It is clear that Gil and Elaine developed the knack for looking past their own noses truly to see and appreciate each other as separate human beings. Unfortunately the ability to empathize is not always easy to come by. Often one's personal troubles block the ability to see anyone or anything else objectively. If we read over Gil and Elaine's interview, it becomes apparent that they share one significant characteristic—both have a strong sense of who they are as individuals separate from their mate. Let us examine more closely this quality of self-awareness, because it is a prerequisite for the development of empathy.

SELF KNOWLEDGE: THE FIRST STEP

Tina recalls having been engaged to Donald for six months when she began having second thoughts about getting married:

> I was feeling that I didn't know enough about what I really wanted to do in life. I loved Donald and didn't want to hurt him, but I didn't want to hurt myself either by cutting off my options too soon. One thing I was sure of: I had to move out of my parents' house and spend time on my own finding out about life. I'm not sure what kind of life Donald imagined for us, and I'm not so sure any more I'd have chosen it even if I had known.

Tina may have felt unsure of what she wanted, but she knew enough about herself to ask, "How can I know who Donald is when I'm not sure who I am?" She seemed to understand intuitively that it is impossible to perceive another clearly without first knowing oneself. Furthermore she was able to see the danger in committing herself in marriage before she knew herself well enough to assess her choice of partners.

All of us feel uncertainty about ourselves, at some times more intensely than others. During periods of deep uncertainty, it is important to be aware of our need for self-exploration, for time to identify what is troubling us, and to clarify our own desires.

Further, we should know at such periods, when the need to look inward is deeply pressing, that our capacity for empathy can be blocked, or sharply limited. Like Tina we must give in to self-exploration at times of uncertainty and try to postpone decisions that involve other people until we are clearer about ourselves.

Still we need not know ourselves fully to enter into an important relationship. Remember Gil and Elaine? It took them a good portion of their early marriage to develop accurate pictures of each other. A marriage is, after all, a commitment to a long-term relationship, and we can expect partners to evolve and change as the marriage goes on, just as we can expect to change ourselves and to sharpen our capacity to see clearly. As long as we can recognize and accept changes in ourselves, it is likely that we will be able to recognize and respond positively to those in our mate. Elaine and Gil's empathetic understanding evolved out of a period of uncertainty and confusion for both. The children were young, the career was just begun, but then, "I began to realize how much his work meant to him..." "I remember looking at the kids and the house in a new way...I started telling her I thought she was doing a terrific job." As one's own self-image becomes clarified, one can emerge from confusion with a greater ability to see one's mate clearly.

A Sense of Self: Being an Individual, Being a Mate

The poet Robert Burns was on target when he said, "O wad some Power the giftie gie us, to see oursels as ithers see us!" You can learn something from the way others see you, and the closer your image of yourself is to that image, the more successful the relationship is likely to be. When you can bear to know who you are, accepting your strengths and weaknesses, appreciating yourself, you are in a good spot to be yourself and let your mate be himself or herself.

In your marriage the more able you are to view your mate from his or her point of view, the more empathy you will have toward your mate's needs and desires. The way you tune in to each other is affected by how well you can separate your own feelings from those of your mate's. If you interpret everything from your own point of view, you are likely to miss the mark in responding to your mate. Achieving a sense of self is tougher than it sounds, but it contributes to the understanding you develop of your mate. How do you do it? You do it by maintaining your individuality while respecting your mate.

Wendy describes her husband:

Marty thought of himself as a tough, rugged individualist, out for number one. But as a husband and father he was a pussycat. He took the time with me, and with the kids too, to lis-

ten to our worries, and yes, he shares the crazy goings on in
his world of finance. We've talked about the different parts of
him, and I think we see that he's both tough and gentle, a
rough competitor and a loving man. For a while he only
showed the one side of his nature, but gradually he let the
warm part come out. Once that happened we got along a lot
better—it was like he was afraid of that softer side—and it was
that part I knew was there that had attracted me 19 years ago.

Thus Marty gradually came to know and accept himself as
a many-faceted creature. he let himself get to know who he
was. The more he knew, the easier it was for him to be more
open to the many dimensions of his wife. When she had
strong opinions, he learned to listen, and instead of taking
her thoughts apart, he tried to understand more about what
she had in mind. He could let go of his own feelings long
enough to understand Wendy's, and he could then offer his
ideas for her consideration. The feeling of being understood,
not necessarily agreed with, is a potent force in developing a
strong sense of trust between partners. From that trust comes
a climate enriched by all the components that heighten the
ability to respond to a mate with empathy.

When mates find themselves closed to each other, holding
tenaciously to their own positions, they rule out opportunities
to participate in the give and take of dynamic marriages. Anyone who wants to enjoy open communication with a mate
needs a capacity for empathy. If you cannot pay attention to
what your mate wants, if you rejoice in verbally knocking him
or her down, you probably are not finding your marriage rewarding. You need to spend time asking yourself, "What's
cooking inside of me that I can't stand diversity?" It probably
would be helpful to look at what is so provocative to you.
What is so threatening that you need to demolish your mate?
If the answers do not come, you might need some professional help to stop the pattern. Your lack of empathy for your
mate may be a stumbling block worth getting rid of since it
deprives you of a satisfying relationship.

Things Inside Us

Some of us grow into adults who never feel satisfied by
what we get from our mates. It always feels like not enough;
no matter how hard our mates try to please us, it just does

not feel good enough. For such insatiable people, it becomes a frustrating experience, trying to hold onto one's own good feelings while also trying to respond to one's mate's needs—as Jean explains:

> How can I understand Bob's desires when I get so little satisfaction myself? It's as though there's a big hole, and no matter what attention Bob tries to give me, it never feels full enough. How can I be aware of his needs with my own gnawing away inside me? At times I try to let go of my demands, but for me it's very hard. I guess people who feel so dissatisfied with themselves have trouble giving to others. I sure wish I could be more in tune with Bob. I want so much to make him happy, but in some ways I guess I'm very selfish.

Jean is not simply selfish; she is an emotionally deprived woman who usually sees life from her vantage point, having difficulty identifying with someone else's viewpoint. She has so few resources inside herself that it is draining to forego her needs for the sake of her husband. She has trouble experiencing her mate without projecting her feelings onto him. It leads Bob to feel both misunderstood and frustrated in getting through to his wife. Jean's struggle seems clear—how can she know or respond to Bob's feelings when her own feelings are exerting a continual pressure on her? For people like Jean, the only solution is to seek the help of a psychotherapist. Other people, not as deeply hurt as Jean, may have trouble letting go of their points of view in order to feel for their mates. For those people it takes some practicing in differentiating their feelings from those of their mates. We can all use some practice in tuning in to our mates.

COMMON BLOCKS TO EMPATHY

Growing self-knowledge is a general requirement not only for empathy, but also for good emotional and mental health. But in our attempt to understand empathy and ways to develop it, it will be helpful to be more specific in pinpointing blockages within ourselves that commonly interfere with our ability to perceive our mates clearly. The first such impediment is perhaps the most familiar: fears and fantasies that cloud our vision of things as they really are.

Fears and Fantasies

To perceive our mates with reasonable accuracy, we need to look past our wishes and fears about the other person, past our obsolete opinions and old evaluations, and open ourselves to our partners *as they really are, right now.* Fears and fantasies of what could be can have great power over us, and too often they muddy our perception of life as it really is.

Joe is a successful lawyer of 43, who has been married for 20 years to Ally, a high school math teacher now working for her master's degree. Both love the theatre, ballet, concerts, and golf. But Joe also loves to fish. His father often took him fishing when he was a boy, and although he has always loved it, he has hardly gone fishing at all since being married. He has never wanted to take a vacation without Ally, and since fishing bores her to death, they have done other things each year. Recently, though, a friend invited Joe to go trout fishing in Canada for a week, and he was tempted to accept. One evening he broached the subject, a little nervously, to Ally: "Honey, Phil has asked me to go fishing with him the first week in June. I know you have exams then and really don't need me around, so I thought I might take him up on it."

Ally was nonplussed. "You mean you want to go away without me? You've never done that before. I thought we always had such good times together on vacation. If you go with Phil, you'll have less time for our trip to Mexico in August." Though she could not say it out loud, she suddenly felt scared. "I'm getting older," she thought to herself. "He's finally bored with me, wants to wriggle out of spending time with me. This is it." The more she thought about it, the more outlandish her fantasies grew. "Maybe he isn't even going fishing at all. Maybe he and Phil have plans for a wild fling. Or maybe they'll meet some pretty flight attendants in the lounge at the fishing resort." Bravely Ally told Joe to go ahead, to have a good time, but inwardly she was in a state of panic. Joe went on his trip and returned, but Ally never could help thinking of the trip as anything but a breach of faith between them. To Joe it always seemed as if she was actually sorry he had had a good time, and he resented the chip she carried on her shoulder over the issue.

Standing between Ally and Joe was a series of pictures in Ally's mind of what *might* have occurred. What inspired them was a sudden change on Joe's part: the suggestion that he break their custom of taking every trip together. Too often married people gain their sense of security purely from sameness and the ability to predict their mates' behavior. Rather than viewing their partners as developing people, changing as they mature, mates often settle on an image and expect their spouses' behavior to conform to it rigidly. When something unexpected occurs, they are too shattered to realize that what has happened merely represents a change, not necessarily a threat.

Had Ally been able to understand that no one, including Joe, remains static in life, she would have seen that Joe really liked fishing, that he missed it, and that his enthusiasm about the proposed trip had only to do with his own pleasure and nothing to do with his love for her. She would have seen that what was at stake was a part of Joe himself, not their marriage at all. In this context she could have expressed her anxiety about feeling left out without calling their whole marriage into question. Joe in turn could have reassured her that he was not trying to avoid her or to seek another relationship, but simply that he wanted to go fishing. With the air cleared, Joe could have gone off without feeling resentful at Ally's anxiety and Ally could have taken real pleasure in the stories he brought back. And—who knows?—she might even have enjoyed the time alone, eating hamburgers in the student lounge and studying far into the night!

Ally could have learned the value of empathy in her own life if she had been calm enough to reflect on the incident. Three years before, when she had decided to go back to school, all Joe could think of was the young men who would be in her classes and the fascinating professors she would meet. He was sure her decision to return to school was her first step to leaving him. She had been amazed at his reaction, and resented his blindness to her real concerns: to finish the education that had been interrupted by childbearing both to prove to herself that she could do it and to improve her earning power. "After all these years, you don't know me very well," she had argued, "if you really think I want to go to school just to meet other men!"

Life is change. In a successful, lasting marriage, partners expect their mates to change and mature and they try hard not to view change with suspicion. It is important to realize that to remain static is to cease growing. To require one's

partner to comform to rigid preconceived ideas of himself or
herself is to cease seeing one's mate as he or she is. We are
all in a process of becoming. A successful marriage evolves
too, as the partners grow and change.

The Fear of Differences

Dean wonders:

> Sometimes I think Carol ought to find a different kind of man.
> Maybe my mood swings take too much of a toll on my family.
> I'm the kind of guy who, when the sky is clear, looks for clouds
> in the distance. If we plan a vacation, I'm sure my boss will
> suddenly announce that he needs me that week. For me the
> glass remains half empty, while for Carol the glass is always at
> least half full. She sees the good side, she never expects the
> worst. Her good nature is inexhaustible—she's always thinking
> things will work out for the best. I get mad sometimes at how
> different her world is from mine. "How can you feel that way
> and still love me?" I ask. Or worse, "How can I love *you* if you
> feel that way and I disagree so strongly?"

Dean is lucky, for Carol clearly can live with the differences between them. She dares to see what is real for her
husband without giving up what is real for herself. Contrary
to a deeply embedded popular myth, marriage partners need
not agree with each other on every point, as long as they can
recognize both positions as valid and the right of both parties
to hold their own views. Many are the husband and wife who
vote different political tickets and have wildly different tastes,
yet do not feel threatened by the differences, and may even be
stimulated by them. To be able to focus on the partner's
needs in order to understand them, to try to feel what it is
like to be in his or her shoes, is true empathy, and a basic
ingredient of a vigorous marriage. Partners may not always be
pleased by what they know about the differences between
them, but they should be unafraid to know it.

Unexamined Parental Images and
Imperfect Adult Sex Models

All of us bring to our marriages attitudes and beliefs from
childhood that we have carried over, unchallenged, into our
adult lives. Many such attitudes have to do with how we perceive men and women in general, and are often determined to

a great degree by the kinds of people our parents and other significant adults in our childhood were. Such attitudes, if they remain unacknowledged and unexamined, can greatly hamper our ability to perceive our mates as they really are. In a later chapter we explore the topic of parental influence on marriage in more depth. For now let us look at an example of how the image of a parent can affect one's perception of a mate through a woman's description of her husband of 27 years.

> Carl would worry about buying me things; he'd worry all the time. I just couldn't reassure him enough about how happy I was in our marriage. I don't care about things, I'd say. I never really did. I never thought about having a big house or three cars when we married. I just wanted to be with Carl. But even after we had the big house and the three cars, he'd worry that he wasn't a good provider, wasn't making sure we had all we wanted. By this time I had realized something very important. Carl's mother was an unhappy woman, very dissatisfied with her lot in life. She hated worrying about money and always wanted things, expecting them to make life better for her. Carl loved her deeply and dreamed of buying her whatever she wanted, but she died before he was earning enough to do that. I think he grew up believing that for women happiness meant having material possessions. He saw his role as providing the woman in his life with things she craved. But me, I never cared. I loved him. Sometimes he forgets it's me, though. He sees his mother standing here.

All of us, in growing up, must make the complicated shift from loving a parent of the opposite sex when we are very little to loving a peer of the opposite sex sometime in adolescence. If we do not fully accomplish this move, we may, in adulthood, still try to satisfy our childhood fantasies of having the parent for our own. This, in a much simplified form, is a description of the dynamics of Freud's well-known theory of the Oedipus complex.

Nearly a century after Freud offered his theories to the world, many of his ideas remain controversial. Most students of human psychology do, however, accept the notion that there is a time in children's lives, usually between ages four and six, when they especially love the parent of the opposite sex. "Mommy, when I grow up I'm going to marry you," says the five-year-old boy, and he means it.

The oedipal triangle exists for all of us, not just for Carl, and it has long been recognized as bringing problems to the marital relationship. Unresolved oedipal conflicts can cause us to behave in ways that are inappropriate to our present circumstances, interfering with our relationships with our mates and blurring our perception of them. But two caring adults can become aware of the hidden causes of their perceptions and behavior. They can modify their behavior by talking about their feelings, as Marion and Carl eventually did, and by helping each other sort out misperceptions. This can happen between two people who trust each other enough to reveal their deepest feelings to each other. In some cases psychotherapy can make this process easier; in others only therapy can enable a person to become aware of unconscious feelings. Carl was lucky that Marion realized his predicament and felt confident enough about her own identity to show him—gently, without anger—that he was misperceiving her.

Many of our assumptions about men and women spring from our perceptions of our parents. We all learn how "grown-ups" behave toward one another in our homes and in the homes of people close to us by watching adults closely when we are children. The boy who sees his father come home and kiss his mother every night is likely to imitate this behavior in his own marriage. The girl who sees her mother trying at all costs to avoid conflict with her husband is likely to feel, when she grows up, that avoiding confrontations is the "right" way to behave. In the same way, some people learn by example how adults should not act, perceiving their parents' ways as hurtful and resolving never to perpetuate such behavior.

This way of learning behavior patterns and sex roles is natural and right. Sometimes, though, we fail to leave the classroom, still carrying into our adult lives images of our parents as the models for our own behavior. We may find ourselves acting toward our mates in ways identical to those our parents exhibited—even when we intensely dislike the pattern and have sworn never to repeat it. Michael, in an interview about why he started therapy, gives us a good idea of how this internal conflict feels.

Cheryl and I would come to a point in an argument when suddenly I couldn't talk about it any more. I'd hit the table so that the plates jumped, yell "All right, that's enough," and walk out. I hated doing it, knew it would only make things worse, but I never could seem to help it. Not being able to control my temper was driving me crazy—especially when I saw what it was doing to Cheryl. She'd back off for days like a scared rabbit. I decided I had to talk to somebody.

Michael's outbursts were direct replays of his father's displays at the dinner table. The boy had learned early that slamming the table was a means, however ineffective in the long run, of putting an end to domestic conflict, and he had never developed another way of behaving in an argument. It worked for his father, and, after a fashion, it worked for him. But Michael was not his father, nor was Cheryl his mother. With therapy Michael was able to find a new way to argue and to resolve conflict that was more compatible with his own and his wife's personalities. Until then he remained unable to perceive Cheryl's position in any argument, for the old move— with the old characters—continued to play itself out through him

Preconceptions and Expectations

Another common block to empathy deserves attention. It is a kind of smugness that takes the place of active listening, and is common in long-term relationships such as that of Ken and Maxine.

Ken does know me very well, but perhaps not as well as he thinks he does. Sometimes he won't listen to how I feel because he thinks—he's *sure*—I feel something else. One night last week he noticed that I was quieter than usual, and he said, "What's bothering you, Maxine?" I said, "Nothing, I'm just a little tired." He said, "Oh, no, I know that look. Something's bothering you, I can tell." After a minute he said, "I know what it is. You're mad at Carrie because she forgot to take out the garbage this morning. Come on, it's just a little thing. Forget it." Nothing could have been further from my mind. I hadn't even thought about the incident after it happened. Still Ken felt he'd hit the nail on the head, and went back to reading the paper satisfied that he was right.

Like many people who feel they are smarter than their spouses, Ken underestimated Maxine and was so convinced that he knew her better than she knew herself that he could not give adequate consideration to her feelings. In fact it seems fair to say that all of us, in our continuing effort to emphathize, need to pay attention to our spouses as they are now. Preconceptions formed early in a relationship may well be outdated, and our expectations can be based on an image that no longer corresponds to reality. Others may also miss the mark with their mates because they project their own feelings onto the mate and ignore what is really going on. Still others may be so entangled with armchair psychology that they continually look for hidden meanings, even when none exists.

As yourself: Who is the person I am married to *really*? What is this person like when I am not around? How does my mate perceive himself or herself? Ask these questions not merely to be considerate, but in an effort to participate fully in the adventure of growing and changing side by side. Welcome change in your mate—new attitudes, flashes of humor, new concerns, and evolving beliefs—as inevitable in the eternal process of becoming. In change lies enrichment. For those who choose to grow up and grow old together, the challenge lies in perceiving and enjoying their mates' ever-evolving selves. The following exercises are designed to see how accurately you perceive your mate, and to help you get more in touch with each other.

EXERCISES

The exercises in this section can be fun, and they can help you and your partner determine how accurately you perceive each other. The important thing to remember in performing them is that there are *no right or wrong answers*. There are no ratings. The purpose of the exercises is to stimulate you and your partner to talk about your perceptions of each other, and through these conversations to correct misconceptions that might interfere with your appreciation of each other as you are.

1. Copy the following chart onto two separate pieces of paper. Add or subtract activities if you wish. You and your mate then rate each item with a 1, 2, or 3 for yourself and for the other. The number "1" means you enjoy the activity all or most of the time; "2" means you enjoy it sometimes; and "3" means you enjoy it rarely or never. *Do not look at each other's charts until you both have completed them.*

	I Enjoy:				I Feel My Mate Enjoys:	
1	2	3		1	2	3
____	____	____	Dancing	____	____	____
____	____	____	Working outdoors	____	____	____
____	____	____	Reading	____	____	____
____	____	____	Making love	____	____	____
____	____	____	Going to movies	____	____	____
____	____	____	Going to museums	____	____	____
____	____	____	Arguing	____	____	____
____	____	____	Going to sport events	____	____	____
____	____	____	Watching television	____	____	____
____	____	____	Listening to music	____	____	____
____	____	____	Making things	____	____	____
____	____	____	Hugging	____	____	____
____	____	____	Cooking	____	____	____
____	____	____	Sharing feelings	____	____	____
____	____	____	Eating	____	____	____

When you are both done, compare your charts to determine how closely your answers in the second column correspond to those in your mate's first column, and vice versa. Where you find differences, discuss the reasons that led you to answer as you did, and ask your mate more about his or her self-perception. Listen carefully to the answers. Do not respond to what you think your partner will answer; actively listen to what he or she says.

2. This exercise is based on feelings rather than actions. Before filling in the blanks, feel free to change the list as you see fit. Remember, there are no right or wrong responses. The object of the game is simply to compare perceptions and to provide a basis for discussing them.

	I Feel I Am				I Feel My Mate Is	
1	2	3		1	2	3
____	____	____	Funny	____	____	____
____	____	____	Capable	____	____	____
____	____	____	Dull	____	____	____
____	____	____	Talented	____	____	____
____	____	____	A satisfying mate	____	____	____
____	____	____	Unattractive	____	____	____
____	____	____	Pessimistic	____	____	____

	I Feel I Am				*I Feel My Mate Is*	
---	---	---		---	---	---
1	2	3		1	2	3
———	———	———	Overprotective	———	———	———
———	———	———	Sexually satisfying	———	———	———
———	———	———	Argumentative	———	———	———
———	———	———	Attractive	———	———	———
———	———	———	Happy	———	———	———
———	———	———	Assertive	———	———	———
———	———	———	Defensive	———	———	———
———	———	———	Dominating	———	———	———
———	———	———	Intelligent	———	———	———
———	———	———	Passive	———	———	———
———	———	———	Sad	———	———	———
———	———	———	Optimistic	———	———	———

If after completing these exercises you feel you and your mate misperceived each other, practice! Discuss the responses. Take time to imagine each other as each of you see yourself. You might find the reality to be far more stimulating than the picture you have built from old fantasies, fears, and obsolete perceptions.

3. Concentrate on one area in which your perceptions proved on the charts to be inaccurate. Ask your mate to talk in detail about this part of his or her self-image, using examples and incidents to help you understand. Be alert to the danger of thinking that you are the expert on your mate. Consider the absurdity of that all-too-frequent conversation stopper, "You're wrong about yourself! I know you like a book and you're just plain mistaken about your motives!" Remember, the whole point of the exercise is to test the accuracy of *your* perceptions—perceptions that are apt to be influenced by fears, fantasies, insecurities, unresolved conflicts, and imperfect models. Give your spouse the attention you would give to an acquaintance whom you would like to get to know better. Let your mate surprise you.

You may find yourself delighted and refreshed.

3

MONEY IS MORE THAN DOLLARS

Scratch the surface of a marriage and what do you find? A commitment to the future? That is something to be hoped for. A shared set of values? Maybe. But look again. What do you find for sure? That's right: money.

On one fundamental, highly pragmatic level, a marriage represents a financial arrangement. This is not to say that at the base of all marriages lies the identical financial arrangement. Rather it means that some sort of decision—whether conscious or unconscious, whether satisfactory to both parties or an ongoing source of resentment—has been reached regarding the way money flows into and out of the shared household.

The specifics of the arrangement are nowhere written in stone. They will differ with the couple and they will reflect the natures of the individuals involved as perhaps nothing else can, except possibly their sexual patterns. Some of these specifics regarding money make more sense than others, and these will be treated later in this chapter.

Though no one way to handle money is right for everyone, we can indeed identify a correct approach to the financial arrangement within marriage. Oddly, as the next chapter will confirm, the hallmarks of a healthy approach to money are virtually indistinguishable from those marking a satisfactory sex life within marriage. These hallmarks are:

43

*Openness
*Trust
*Mutual respect
*Attentiveness to detail

The converse of this concept is also true: Where trust, openness, respect, and attentiveness are lacking, financial concerns—as well as other issues within the marriage—are bound to be problematical. In both important areas, money and sex, problems will not solve themselves, and if left untended, will only get worse. It is important to note that at issue here is not the amount of money that comes and goes (we will see in the next chapter that the same is true for sex: the amount, as measured in frequency, has nothing to do with quality). The central issue is pure attitude: what money means to both people, how the partners cope individually and together with too little money (or too much), and what they consider to be worth spending for when financial resources are limited.

LANGUAGE OF MONEY

Debbie talks about money:

> My mom used really to "get" my dad by coming home with all kinds of clothes that looked great on her. They both knew we couldn't afford them, but Mom realized that Dad couldn't resist giving in to her. Mom was sort of punishing him for not making a better living. I think maybe I'm doing some of that with Tom. We keep getting into the hole each month, and I somehow find things I just have to have. I know he wants me to look good and be happy, but there's probably a better way.

Along with Debbie's dawning awareness of the habits she shares with her mother with respect to money comes a new understanding of how people use money to "talk" within families, saying things they do not dare or care to say aloud. We are dealing with a novel interpretation of that old saw "money talks." The idea here is not simply that money can impress some people as nothing else can, but rather that we often use money symbolically to say things we cannot say in words.

People often use their money habits to express unresolved conflicts stemming from childhood—rebellion against tight-fisted parents, perhaps, or against the feeling that their parents bought them off with money while withholding the affection they craved. Or they use money to tell their mates in a roundabout way that something is amiss in the marriage.

Money is symbolic in nature. Currency only stands for value; it has no inherent worth of its own. Therefore it is not surprising that we sometimes use money instead of language as our primary system of symbols. When we cannot say something in words, because the message is too painful, too confusing, too destructive, or too unclear, we often say it with money.

Furthermore, when we are afraid to say what we mean, we are often afraid to *know* what we mean. Therefore we remain unaware of the messages we are delivering every time we overspend, underbudget, or blow the nest egg on a whim.

On the practical level, serious spending or saving problems often result from using money to "talk" in this way, since handling money wisely requires discipline and self-control, which themselves depend on maturity, clarity, and the resolution of inner conflict. This explains why people who are otherwise dependable can act as spendthrifts, misers, or children where money is concerned. When such extreme behavior occurs in a marriage and runs counter to the partner's spending ways, watch out! Expect fireworks, ongoing grousing, or repressed resentment that eventually becomes rage, depending on the level of free-flowing communication between the two mates.

What is so hard about learning to spend money in a reasonable way? What are the inner drives that lead to irresponsible behavior in people who are otherwise dependable? They are internal messages insisting on being transmitted, old baggage urgently requiring attention, problems shoved under the rug long ago and never allowed to come out They represent the imperative of our maturing process: You cannot grow up without tackling the tasks of each stage. That is, you cannot move on to the next level of maturity until you finish the business of the one before. If you do not finish, that unfinished business will fight for your attention where it is most likely to attract it: in your checkbook or in your bedroom. We cover the sexual forum in the next chapter. Here we look at common reasons why otherwise responsible, dependable people make messes of the financial realities they face with their spouses.

The chief lesson in this chapter is: *Take the symbolism out of money.* Money is simply money, a means of acquiring food, shelter, security, pleasure, and not a language or a means of controlling others. Though it is easy to use money to express our inner selves, doing so confuses the issue almost immediately. Thus even people who are committed to being honest and objective are often sabotaged in their efforts to see their financial situations clearly if they still have unresolved problems stemming from an earlier time in their lives.

Let us look at some examples of how money talks in this undertone, confusing the present with messages from the past.

Consider Daniel, a 46-year-old attorney, who acts like a pouting 12-year-old when his wife explains that they just do not have enough money for him to buy that latest stereo component. He is feeling just as he did as a kid when his parents scolded him for blowing his entire savings on 150 sticks of bubble gum.

Quite simply this man's sense of spending has hardly matured over the past 40 years. He is still resisting and rebelling against his parents, throwing a fit if he cannot have something he likes, instantly viewing his wife as the enemy, someone to be distrusted and defied.

Even the objective facts as they show on his bank statement do not convince Daniel that the expenditure would be a mistake. He is still too young inside to concern himself with statements and balances and such. All he knows is that he wants that piece of equipment. And he knows that throwing a tantrum is an effective way to get it. That sort of emotional blackmail worked on his parents, so why should it not work on his wife? No reason at all! He throws the tantrum—by shouting down his wife's reasonable objections—and runs out to buy his beloved component. When overdrawn notices start showering the family in the middle of the subsequent month, Daniel cannot understand it. He never gives another thought to the purchase he made, but instead gives his wife a very stern lecture about cutting back in her grocery buying.

Daniel has a problem. But the fact is, marriage makes it his wife Pamela's problem too. Pamela meanwhile has a completely different history with money, and brings a very different set of baggage to the marriage.

Pamela's father, a mathematics professor, fell in love with a student and left the family when Pam was 13. Until then the family had lived a typical upper-middle-class life, there was never a whisper of financial insecurity in the house. But when the father left, Pam's mother had to go to work, after being out of the labor market for nearly 20 years. She was lucky to find a job as an administrative assistant in a nonprofit agency for "displaced homemakers" like herself, a job she liked very much but that paid practically minimum wage. The fear of poverty invaded Pam and her mother's household and never left. They always had the sense that they were living on the edge of a chasm, with certain death the sure result if the family went off the edge. Pam never lost this feeling of controlled panic around money; it was the invisible dowry she brought to her marriage with Daniel.

Now every time their bank balance dipped after one of Daniel's tantrums, Pam felt the old fear of poverty well up in her, and she became tight-lipped and preoccupied. It did not help that she also feared, unconsciously, that Daniel would leave her as her father had left her mother. Thus violent insecurity assailed her at the very hint of a fluctuation in the family's bank balance. Needless to say, the outward expressions of this insecurity, and her anxious attempts to hide them, made her hard to live with.

The objective facts in the case were that Daniel made a very comfortable living and could afford an occasional extravagance, but too much money was tied up in investments. Hence what was experienced on a month to month basis was partially a cash-flow problem that could be remedied by some practical shifts in their resources.

During a luncheon reunion with an old college room-mate Pam heard her friend discuss her own financial bind and she realized that she and Daniel were nowhere near the edge of poverty that she was feeling. Her new perspective gave her a jolt, and she decided to get some professional help to sort out her reactions. It gradually helped her shake off her fear and enabled her to deal more effectively with Daniel. Some time later when Daniel had the urge to defy her, bulldozing an unnecessary expenditure through, instead of freezing up and panicking, Pam was able to offer suggestions as to when they could work the expenditure into their budget. Without the fear of poverty and abandonment, Pam was ready to engage her husband in reasonable discussion. Daniel eventually joined his wife in therapy and as the origins of his hostile reactions were explored his anger abated and his behavior changed. Both partners now had the chance to experience money as a resource, not a weapon.

Pam came to understand that this was so during the course of a reunion lunch with her old college roommate Gwen, who really did live on the edge of poverty. As Pam listened to her friend discuss the bind she was in financially, she realized that from Gwen's point of view she and Daniel must seem unimaginable well off. This new perspective gave her a jolt, and she decided to get some professional help. To sort out her behavior. It gradually helped her shake off her fear and see things as they were—as figures on a page. Some time later when Daniel had the urge to defy her, bulldozing an unnecessary expenditure through, instead of freezing up and panicking, Pam gently suggested he take the cash from one of his holding accounts so as not to disrupt the household budget. Done! Both partners had what they wanted, and Pam at least had a new lease on life.

WHEN BELLS RING THE LIGHTS COME ON

As with many of the issues covered in this book, a realistic approach to money often requires some rigorous seeking after self-knowledge. Marriage often showcases characteristics that the partners had managed to hide from themselves throughout their single lives. A life-long spending pattern, for example, often reveals itself with the decision to marry. The cost of the wedding upon which the couple decides, the extravagance of the honeymoon, and the size and location of the first apartment all indicate things about the financial attitudes each partner brings to the marriage without knowing it.

Interestingly, the compromise the partners strike on these very early decisions often becomes the theme of the marriage, as far as financial matters are concerned. This can be unfortunate since, as will become clear in later chapters, the communication skills essential to solid decision making often take practice—sometimes years of it—to perfect. Newlyweds who are just beginning to feel their way into a style of communication may arrive at some less-than-satisfactory financial arrangements that they never renegotiate.

Moreover conditions change as the years go by: financial responsibilities become more numerous as a rule, especially as the family grows, income shifts, and living arrangements change. Of equal importance are the changes that occur in the national economy or within the particular sector in which the family earns its living.

For all these reasons, it is important to note that *flexibility* is a necessary characteristic of all financial arrangements, inside and outside marriage. And linked to flexibility, by necessity, is *clarity*—for without the power to observe objective conditions clearly, one can never make the adjustments necessary to adapt to the inevitable changes in conditions.

As an example, one couple who came to see me was in a constant state of anxiety and self-deprecation because their small income no longer seemed to cover their expenses even though their children had moved out and their food budget had been cut in half. Not once in all their hopeless arguments on the subject had they considered the reality of rampant inflation. They blamed themselves, they blamed each other, but they could never look outward and blame the economy. Clarity on the objective facts—in this case, the double-digit inflation that was plaguing the whole country—gave them a new understanding and relieved them of their crippling self-blame.

Another common problem is habitual self-indulgence never brought under control. Some couples begin their marriages, in a burst of youthful exuberance, at a level of spending just slightly higher than their earning level. When they remain inflexible and unable to address the problem clearly, this pattern may plague them throughout their marriage. Such a couple is never free from debts, and often must pay enormous interest charges, which add to the indebtedness. The two are usually amazed at the relief they experience when they finally manage to break the cycle. One simple solution—given that the necessary clarity, openness, and trust exists between them—is to declare a temporary moratorium on buying. There will be no more credit-card charging until an agreed-upon amount is paid off.

"OUR" MONEY VERSUS "MY" MONEY

The fact is, financial problems are practical matters with practical solutions, as long as they are not serving to communicate symbolically what the partners cannot or will not say in language. But even where symbolism is not a major factor, finding the practical solution requires discussion and compromise, since people are so different and personal history has such a dramatic effect on attitudes toward money.

Let us look at Mark and Susan. Mark likes to play with money: he has always been good at it and the risks he has taken have usually paid off. His parents were supportive of the gambles he took as a young man and reinforced his belief that investing was a form of play. Therefore, when he announced excitedly to Susan on their honeymoon that he had "taken a flier" on a stock investment and that great riches might be theirs, he was mystified and disappointed by her sour response. After trying to inspire her with the spirit of the game, he got angry, and this anger simmered below the surface throughout their 18-year marriage, springing up full-blown every time they disagreed on a financial risk. Here is what he said in therapy, where they had gone to discuss other pressures:

> Sue's just a dud when it comes to money. She's never worked, and she doesn't understand anything having to do with numbers. Her idea of a safe bet is to squirrel away as much money as she can. No way would she agree to take a chance on losing anything. But she just doesn't know. Everything we have today I've acquired by taking chances.

Now let us see Sue's side. As a child Sue had watched an uncle lose every hope of financial independence by the same method—taking chances. Whereas Mark had never lost a big gamble in his life, this uncle went from cocky to pathetic over the course of Sue's childhood and was a drain on her father until he died. Is she a "dud" or is she providing the point of view that is missing in her husband's approach? After all the stakes are a lot higher for a family man than for a free-as-a-bird teenager investing his graduation money. Sue wanted to influence the action, since she would be sharing in the consequences.

The work these two had to do was to move away from the opposite extremes they represented and toward a common ground where compromise would be possible. The next step would be negotiation to reach an acceptable level of living.

One principle dominates when marriage partners are negotiating financial understandings: If the arrangement is to work, both partners have to view the money in a marriage, whether earned by one or both parties, as *our* money. *We* have X amount of money to spend on *ourselves, our* children, *our* house, *our* pleasures.

All right, you say, but what do we do when we have different needs, different pleasures, even children from a different marriage? The answer is the same: *we* work out solutions that accommodate the differences.

"Sure" objects Harry, "but if it's all ours, then what's mine? Can't I have anything that belongs just to me? It's as though I'm giving up who I am if everything I own my wife owns too." Harry worries a lot about losing his identity, but he is especially concerned about his sense of autonomy and freedom when it comes to making financial decisions. He needs to understand that once the partners agree upon a level of spending, both can still go out independently to buy the things they want, as long as they stay within the agreed-upon limits.

The key to such understanding is open discussion, free from symbolism. "Our" money decisions, made through compromise, lead to agreements to spend in particular ways. Mark and Sue worked out their problem, with the help of a therapist. They came to agree specifically on a "reasonable" level of risk. During the course of therapy, Sue was able to lay to rest the ghost of her unsuccessful uncle by acknowledging that Mark had a lot more going for him by way of brains, experience, and capital. Mark, meanwhile, could admit that he had hated Sue's "killjoy" attitude from the beginning, and sometimes went ahead with iffy deals just to punish her for having it. Once the ventilating and exploration of pent-up feelings were over, the discussion took the form of realistic negotiations over a figure that both partners could live with as a reasonable level of risk.

THE SECOND TIME AROUND

Couples who have had prior marriages may find themselves with additional problems, wanting to protect a prior nest egg, making sure there is enough control over the money, wanting discretion to spend their own earnings. Consider the impact on Jennifer.

Jennifer had always had trouble getting her first husband to agree to give her adequate money for clothing. In those days she did not work and was totally dependent financially.

> James would look into my closet and tell me that I had plenty of clothes and that he couldn't understand how I could possibly want more—"How many blouses can you wear at one time?" And what could I say? When I said I needed new things each season, he thought I was out of my head. He didn't like to shop, to wear new things, and always had more "noble" places he thought the money should go. It made it tough, because I often felt so selfish. Well, no more. I won't ever live like that again!

She vowed that she would never give up her financial autonomy if she were ever to marry again. After six years of independent living, Jennifer was determined to maintain control of her earnings when she remarried. She lacked any conviction that she and her husband could work out mutually acceptable joint decisions about spending.

The idea of splitting all the money equally was out of the question for Jennifer on another score. She no longer had full faith that marriage is forever, and had a strong desire to protect the money she had accumulated earlier in her life. She also felt that since she and her current husband both earned a hefty income, they should agree to share their common expenses and then retain some of the excess in separate accounts. Each could spend this money with absolute discretion as he or she saw fit.

That sounds neat, logical, and can work well much of the time, as long as both partners share the money fairly equally. But how much is "discretionary" money? Is an illness of one not the concern of the other? Would unexpected bills be paid out of both people's accounts? What if one person spends all discretionary money on fun things and then, when the plumbing goes expects the partner to come up with the money?

Discretionary money then is the dispensable money—$500, $1000, $5000 a year (depending on your income level)—that each person enjoys for independent purchases, as long as *both* agree that such money is "extra". It gets more complicated when one of the partners earns more than the other. It creates two separate life-styles. One can afford a two-week vacation at Lake Louise while the other is able to manage only a weekend in Barstow.

The better way, all around, is to think of *currently earned* money as "ours." It may be sensible to protect an estate earlier developed with prenuptial agreements, or to make it clear that certain money, perhaps from prior inheritances, should go to one's children, but in general a marriage works better when you share a life-style. It pays to take the time to understand each other's feelings, to allow leeway for different values, to accommodate to each other's needs. Each partner has to feel the respect of the other and relinquish ideas about the "right way" to spend.

MONEY AS REWARD

Very commonly, in its symbolic function money serves as a "reward" in marriage, which brings up the complex issues of power and equality. We are all familiar with the situation in which the husband, expressing his delight over how well his wife entertained his business associates, for instance, gives her an extra bit of money to use as she likes. She then feels like a child being rewarded by daddy for "being such a good girl." Where such is the entrenched pattern, the wife's sense of autonomy and maturity has been permanently traded for bits of "extra" reward money.

The converse pattern exists in some households, too, where the man is granted license for some extravagance when, like "a good little boy," he performs some household chore or takes over the child care for the day.

It is true that adults like to be rewarded as much as children do, and there is certainly nothing wrong with people showing their appreciation to others by giving gifts. The issue, though, is that a trade-off is involved. A gift is freely given, but payment implies goods or service in return. Take the idea of trade-off a little farther, and it becomes an issue of control.

MONEY AS CONTROL

Throughout history people with money have used it to dominate those with less. And since ancient times, it has been common knowledge that money often corrupts the possessor, debasing those who control it. The ancient Orientals dubbed gold "the excrement of hell," quite effectively calling attention to the danger inherent in growing too attached to money.

A generation or two ago, men with controlling behavior who made all the financial decisions in the household were considered to be acting in ways that were "natural and right." In those days, and in all those preceding that time, men owned their wives, and the question of equal partners simply never arose. It was considered completely correct that the man have total control, not just over finances, but over every detail, every decision, pertaining to his household, from hearth and home to children and wife.

Today, however, we consider such marital inequality to be pathological, as clearly wrong in its denial of basic human rights as racism or other forms of prejudicial hatred. But despite our generally enlightened view, details often escape our notice. Consider, for example, the men who dole out scant sums "for the household" while amassing large sums of which their wives have only the vaguest knowledge or the women who feel that anything they earn belongs exclusively to them while arguing their husband's earnings should be shared equally. At the source of such skullduggery is a need to dominate others and the fear of being denigrated by them.

One phenomenon that appears to be a particularly common hanger-on from those older, more unfair days is the monitoring of wives' expenditures by eagle-eyed husbands. This problem crops up in certain households no matter whether the wives work or not. Where it occurs the wives are generally responsible for keeping the house running and for making all the domestic purchases, but the husbands are apt to question the cost of any item and feel that they have the authority to veto any purchase the wife makes. Barbara is such a wife.

Bob would never let me spend $30 on running shoes. He thinks my running is stupid—a fad that will pass. But I'm really getting into it now, training for my first marathon. I'm still running in my tennis shoes, though my toes are starting to peep out of them. Bob always looks at all the bills, and I often feel guilty about spending anything extra on myself, or even on the kids.

Bob's attitude toward his wife's growing interest in running is demeaning and disrespectful. That is one problem. An equally thorny problem is Barbara's acceptance of this lesser position, as evidenced in the guilt she feels at spending on what she calls "extras"—things she and her children might need or enjoy. She subscribes to the philosophy that if the man is the total breadwinner, he gets the veto on every expenditure. Reinforcing this belief is a gnawing guilt that she herself has never contributed financially to the family's livelihood.

Women who feel guilty about not earning money, or not earning as much as their husbands, suffer from a lack of clarity on the objective facts. Like Barbara, they often dismiss the contributions they make as homemakers, mothers, and wives. They see themselves as dependent by nature, but in fact they make it possible for their husbands to go out into the world to earn a living while still enjoying the security and comfort of home and family. Overall they, and their husbands, make the mistake of thinking that equality means contributing exactly the same amount in exactly the same way. In fact partners do not duplicate the labor; they share it, each contributing in his or her area of expertise so that all the work gets done.

Further, many people of both sexes accept the potent and destructive myth that personal worth is related to dollar-earning power. "If the marketplace doesn't value my skills, they must not be worth anything at all," they reckon. The result is a phenomenon we encounter often in this book: low self-esteem, a condition that feeds itself over time and can eventually extinguish the person's initiative in improving his or her life. In households where a husband holds sway on all financial matters and the wife, like Barbara feels undeserving of the necessities related to her most driving interests, the wife's slow downward spiral into diminishing self-esteem is inevitable.

Where unequal control is an issue, the first step toward a solution is acknowledging the problem. This step will not be easy for one who perpetually feels the weaker partner in an unequal match, but knowing the dynamics of the situation can help. Where you are a wife whose expenditures are under scrutiny, find out how housework is valued in some of the comparable-pay studies done recently. Think realistically about your contributions when your husband was in school or training for his present position, and ask him outright how much he values his home life and the extra parenting you have done as the at-home caretaker.

Remember, there is much in our society to reinforce that dangerous myth that personal worth is related to earning power. You have to be sure of yourself to buck it, which means you have to turn inward and assess yourself honestly and scrupulously. If your values are shaky, you are on dangerous ground, as one of my clients was when I asked her what she got by staying in her terribly unhappy marriage. "Why?" she answered, amazed that I'd asked. "Why shouldn't I stay with him? I have the three M's, what more do I need?" "The three M's?" I asked, "Sure, money, a mink, and a Mercedes!" Had I been able at the time I might have urged her to trade the three M's for the three S's: self-acceptance, self-respect, and self-assurance. I'm not sure it would have made an impression. She had a lot of work to do to gain back her self-esteem, and no motivation to do so.

But what about the other side of the problem? How does the breadwinner break his or her attachment to the bread in the interests of equal spending power within the marriage? Arlene, is the sole breadwinner for her family while her husband goes to medical school. She has a good job at good pay, and is even footing the bill for Mike's tuition. "Why shouldn't I decide how to spend it?" she asks. "After all, I work tremendously hard earning it, so I don't want anybody telling me how it should be allotted." Her sentiment echoes that of many men and women who work hard, and often dislike their jobs to boot. People in this position need to develop a way of sharing in decisions, allowing each other enough autonomy to spend reasonably without discussing and agreeing on every purchase. The answer is equal power *and* equal autonomy.

"Equal?" cries Rob. "There's no such thing with Sharon. She can talk me into anything! Her logic is so incredible that I end up agreeing to things I know I don't want, but who can win?"

That is just the point: nobody should win. Rob and Sharon need to understand that successful money negotiation should end with both partners feeling good about the financial decisions they reach together.

Where agreement on the level of living and spending seems impossible, I strongly advocate bringing in an arbitrator, in the person of a financial counselor, or a therapist. The issue is so basic, and the anger stirred by a lack of agreement can be so destructive if left to fester, that resolving conflict over money is essential to successful married life.

Once the partners are in general agreement about the level of spending they can afford, then the specific items—a new suit, a tennis racquet, a book, a movie—become separate decisions made within the environment shaped by the fundamental agreement.

Let us reserve the mommy and daddy roles for guiding our children, and work to approach the topic of money together as adults with a grasp of the facts.

EXERCISES

Money is a major problem for most people. Use these exercises to stimulate a dialogue between you and your mate to try to understand his or her position. Changes can usually be made if you look for reasonable agreement.

1. Answer the questions as honestly as you can, separately. Then compare your answers and talk about the things that trouble you in your views about money handling. See if you can help your mate understand the way in which you are affected by money decisions in your family.

1 = all or most of the time

2 = sometimes

3 = rarely or never

	Most	*Some*	*Rarely*
I feel our income covers our necessities.	1	2	3
I feel my mate resents my not working.	1	2	3

	Most	Some	Rarely
I feel an equal authority in how our money is spent.	1	2	3
I want more input in money decisions.	1	2	3
It is hard for me to spend money.	1	2	3
My mate and I disagree about how our money should be spent.	1	2	3
I feel we plan well for our future.	1	2	3
I feel my mate is extravagant.	1	2	3
I feel my mate is too lax in spending.	1	2	3
I would like to live within an agreed-upon budget.	1	2	3
I dislike budgets.	1	2	3
I would like to discuss our spending more clearly.	1	2	3

	Yes	No
I would like some "discretionary" money.	Yes	No

If the answer is "yes", discuss with your mate.

The following is a sample of a way to look at your spending and how it relates to your income.

	Fixed Expenses
Rent/mortgage	$
Food	$
Utilities	$
Phone	$
Schooling	$
Insurance	$
Auto	$
Other	$_____
Subtotal	$

	Variable Expenses
Clothes	$
Charge accounts	$
Recreational/entertainment	$
Vacations	$
Luxuries	$
Savings	$
Investments	$
Other	$_____
Subtotal	$

Optional

Discretionary Fund: this is a fund for each partner, based on "extra" money that is available for which autonomous control is enjoyed, for example, $500 a year, $1000 a year, $5000 a year. This fund can change, based on income and needs, and can be most helpful for couples who disagree about what might constitute a luxury or a necessity.

Income: _____   Outgo: _____

If your outflow is greater than your income, you may need to consider ways to reduce the spending or increase the earnings. Husbands and wives can share the economic and household burdens. If you are continually spending more than you can earn, you may benefit from consulting a finance counselor or a psychotherapist.

Above all enjoy the money you have.

4
SEXUALITY
Keeping the Spark Alive

With BEAUTIFUL BODIES
beamed at us from every billboard, movie screen, and television comedy, one question periodically haunts the mind of nearly everyone involved in an intimate relationship: How can we ensure sexual satisfaction, how keep the spark alive?

This question should be of concern to all marriage partners. But our sex- and youth-oriented society does not help us approach the concern realistically. Far from reassuring those who care about maintaining or improving the quality of sexual intimacy within marriage, the media seem to imply that sex within marriage is bound to grow stale and that the real sexual excitement is to be found in the singles bars, in partner swapping, or in frequent affairs. We get the idea that everyone but ourselves is living in a state of constant sexual excitement broken only by frequent periods of blissful satisfaction.

These myths are blatantly untrue. Our supposedly sexually free society is just as troubled about sex as in earlier, supposedly more repressed eras. The notion that sexuality is somehow deepened or improved when we become more sophisticated or have a wide assortment of partners is erroneous. And the implication that you have to be young and beautiful to have a satisfying sex life is equally inaccurate. If you took a poll of the people in psychotherapists' waiting rooms around the country, you would find a great many "sophisticated," "experienced," and young, good-looking singles, along with a large number of married people of all ages and appearances, puzzling through the problems of integrating sexual gratification with intimacy, trust, and self-respect.

Still, if you talked with married couples, you would discover that sexuality within marriage raises specific concerns, not necessarily more urgent than those of the unmarried, but different. Single people struggle with problems of loneliness, casual sex with changing partners, availability of partners, and poor self-regard in the sexual arena. Married people are most often troubled by a fear that sex with their partners will lose its initial excitement and become routine, and that both mates may soon be too bored to bother with lovemaking at all. How can they sustain sexual interest in their partners over the long term? How can they continue to stimulate their partners' interest in them? How can they cope with lost youth? These questions are troubling and exceedingly widespread. Fortunately, when we wipe away the glaze of adventure and overstimulation created by the media, we can find answers to these questions and solutions to the problems.

UPS AND DOWNS IN THE MARRIAGE BED

Many studies have documented the fact that the frequency of sexual intercourse diminishes as couples remain together over time. Typically partners who began their marriage spending hours in bed every day find that over the years the frequency of their sexual episodes drops to once or twice a week, or several times a month. Furthermore our study revealed that though sexual satisfaction most of the time was a universal characteristic of successful long-term marriage, partners felt a fluctuation in their sexual interest in one another, over the years. They reported periods of greater and lesser sexual interest, though the overall satisfaction appeared to point upward as the children moved out of the house and spouses had more time and energy for each other. A diagram of the pattern of sexual interest between long-term partners (not including old age) might look something like Figure 1.

Thus the fact that a couple is mismatched for an evening or a week or a month does not necessarily indicate that their sex life is no good, that their marriage is a failure, or that they do not love each other. All people experience some doubts during a long-term marriage, some fleeting, some more lasting. The modern emphasis on sexuality and on the more-is-better ethic can cause unnecessary anxiety about such inevitable developments between long-term partners. The antidote is to understand that fluctuations in desire, intensity, and sexual frequency are normal and universal.

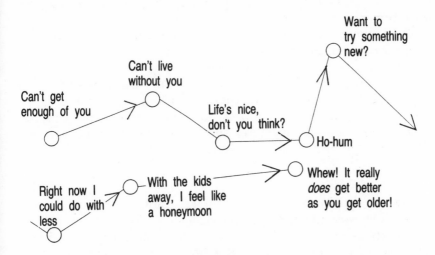

Figure 1
Pattern of sexual interest—long-term partners.

WHAT IS SEXUAL SATISFACTION?

We have identified what long-term sexual satisfaction is not: flashy, frequent, youth-and-beauty-oriented sex. But what, over the long run, is sexual satisfaction?

Where two people feel affection or love for each other, sex

is an important means of expressing those feelings. The successful communication of loving feelings through sex imparts a measure of satisfaction to both partners. The California study indicates that sexual satisfaction consists of two more identifiable components as well. The first component is familiar.

1. *Sexual satisfaction is purely subjective. It exists in a long-term relationship when both mates agree that is exists.*

No outside standards can contradict the partners' certainty that they have achieved a style of relating to each other sexually that is fulfilling to them both. But even this statement begs the question. What, after all, is meant by "fulfilling"? The answer yielded by the study is that sexual satisfaction is rooted in that complex feeling we have for some human beings but not for others: trust.

2. *Thus, a basic requirement for sexual satisfaction in a long-term marriage is trust.*

The sexual relationship reflects feelings of love, anger, disappointment, and so on, and satisfaction will fluctuate with the presence or absence of these emotions. But basic to an enduring sexual relationship is each partner's sense that he or she can risk experiencing these negative feelings without losing the other's love and trust.

Trust

We can best examine the complex emotion of trust by example. Let us compare two marriages, the first characterized by a distinct lack of trust in the sexual realm, and the second by a positive sense of mutual trust in sexual matters.

Ann and Jack were married for 19 years, and in all that time Ann had suspicions about the role she played in Jack's sex life.

> Well, you know, he never really asked me whether I enjoyed the way he made love. It never seemed to concern him. At first I guess I wanted to talk about it, but things were different then about sex. I have to admit I never knew until a few years ago that women could feel pleasure in sex, you know, the way men do, and to tell you the truth I don't know how much Jack knew, or knows now, about women's bodies. Whatever he knows, he never seems to care; it's always been his show, and quick, like he wants to do it and be finished quickly, with the finish all that counts. I suspect he stopped loving me that way

a long time ago. Sure, I remember when he did love me and couldn't wait to go to bed with me. I held out during our engagement but he'd kind of make jokes about it and worry me that he wouldn't go through with the marriage unless I went, you know, all the way. I finally did, and he seemed to love it. I thought it would get better for me after a while, after he cooled down and began to see that it wasn't so great for me. But I never could bring myself to tell him out loud—I didn't want to hurt him, didn't want him to feel I was being too critical. It was different when I got married; you heard an awful lot about "the male ego" then, and how your marriage depended on not bruising it and on making him feel like he was "manly" enough. I never did get around to telling him that our sex life left me cold. It always seemed easier to just let it go.

Now meet Sheila, married to Manny for 27 years.

I remember making love with Manny for the first time when we were just kids, 19 years old. He'd had some sexual encounters before but I was a virgin. After we made love that day he was just ecstatic—shouting around, laughing, waving his feet in the air. But I just hated it and he could tell when he looked at me it hadn't been any good at all. That pricked his balloon. I told him I hadn't felt *anything* and was really disappointed after the big buildup sex had received for so long. We were both puzzled and, well, you know what we did? Typical of some engaged college students, we got a book! And we read it together, poring over the pictures—no photos in those days, it was all diagrams and medical-type language. To tell you the truth, though, looking at those pictures with Manny really turned me on, and after some time trying new things, I had an orgasm. Then we were both laughing and carrying on, and it's been like that ever since. We've really grown up together sexually.

Things got a little slow between us sometimes. When the kids were all young (they're a year apart and there are three of them) was the worst time for us sexually. We were tired a lot and worried a lot and I especially felt the opposity of sexy. But now we're closer than ever—and, you know, come to think about it, we still read sexy books together, and look at sexy pictures after all these years!

Finally here is Michael, whose story encompasses both kinds of relationships.

I was married briefly in my early 20s and then separated. I met Jeannie (my second wife) when I was 25. We married the next year and have been living together ever since, for 30 years now. My first wife was a beautiful woman, but vain and mean, I see now. Shortly after we married, I started having bouts of jealousy followed by impotence. I suspected that she was seeing other men and accused her of it. Then when I'd want to make love to her I couldn't get an erection. She'd laugh at me, make snide jokes about it during the day, and she'd never answer me when I asked her about other men. Then I lost my job, and after that I was impotent all the time. She just went out four or five nights a week, and of course she was gone all day earning our bread and butter. Finally she just left and had divorce papers sent to me through the mail.

Her leaving was the best thing that ever happened to me, though I didn't feel that way then. I was wrecked, left with no job, no wife, and the suspicion that I would be impotent for life. I met Jeannie on a blind date and I remember I was so scared she'd see what a mess I was I could hardly introduce myself. But we had a great time, and I remember being surprised in the weeks after our date about having sexy thoughts about Jeannie and feeling stirrings. We didn't actually have intercourse until we had dated a few months, and I didn't feel completely relaxed about it until I told Jeannie all about my first wife and about her leaving me and what led up to it. I remember buying a bottle of wine and sitting down with it and saying, "Look, I want to tell you all about this and drink wine until I've told you everything." So by the time we got to the hard part, about my being impotent, I was feeling pretty free. She didn't laugh—remember, I was used to being laughed at about that. But Jeannie listened seriously, and when we made love after that talk, it went without a hitch. We've had our ups and downs, but we're still going strong after 30 years.

The essence of trust, as these stories reveal, is the ability to be honest and open without fear. Thus trust leads to intimacy—in bed and out. Often one needs time and experience together to develop trust in someone, particulary when sexual matters are involved. Consider what Bette has to say about this.

When Don and I were first married, he let me know that he wanted oral sex. I didn't like the idea at all. I felt kind of ashamed even talking about it. I knew I should be uninhibited and free with Don—after all, he was my husband—but I'd grown up thinking oral sex was perverted, and that feeling prevented me from figuring out whether I actually found it exciting or not. But lately I've been hearing lots more about different kinds of sex and everybody seems to agree that oral sex isn't as perverted as all that. I was raised in the '50s. We did a lot of petting, but to me at least oral sex was even more out of line than intercourse. Things are easier now, though, and I really started thinking about it. So one morning when we were making love I just moved down the bed and opened my mouth around Don's penis. I almost laughed I was so self-conscious, and I knew he was so surprised he was just dying, but I really wanted to find out what the fuss was all about and whether we might like doing it, whether it might spice things up for us. Needless to say Don was ecstatic, not just because he really liked the feeling, but because he could see I felt a lot freer about things. Since then we've both loosened up a lot. It's that first step that's hard, because your husband expects you to be the way you've always been. It takes a lot of nerve to surprise him, but I'm getting nervier all the time! It's him, really, who is helping me with that. I could never have done it if I thought he'd be angry or make fun of me for breaking out of my mold.

One outgrowth of a trusting relationship is the ability to take risks without the fear of losing the partner's love and injuring the basic relationship. Bette was able to take a risk after long considering it, but Gloria and Stan's story reveals the process of the growth of trust in the sexual area over time. Says Gloria:

Stan saw himself as something of a ladies' man when I met him. I was impressed with his demeanor, and when we married, swept away by his prowess in bed—I thought I was pretty experienced, and for those times I was. I had been married before and loved making love. But Stan was a great lover, tender, patient, and very direct about finding out what I liked. I just couldn't believe how considerate he was, and how willing to delay his own pleasure while he paid attention to me. After a few months of marriage, though, it started getting to me. I want to give him as much pleasure as he was giving me. I wanted to touch and stroke him while he was stroking me, but he'd push my hands away gently and go back to arousing me. One night, after we'd been drinking a little, I tried to kiss his penis and he just abruptly stopped and rolled over, kind of mad. I couldn't understand what was up, but I finally got it out of him: he couldn't stand to be touched, said his penis was too sensitive, that he'd rather we just keep it the way we were, with him stimulating me manually and orally and he getting his pleasure from orgasm during intercourse. I agreed, but it really bugged me. I didn't like being on a one-way street. I wanted to receive *and* give.

The issue came up every so often from then on, and I think I got madder about it as time went on because I felt that Stan's dislike of being touched sexually stemmed from his need to be in control of our sex life, the one who was in charge but never lost his own cool. What was that cool he was preserving so hard? I never let the subject completely drop. I'd bring it up from time to time and make him talk to me, always telling him that I wanted to fondle him because I loved him, that I wanted to give him back some of the pleasure he gave me. He seemed afraid of it somehow, but once in a while he'd relent, and I'd be careful but try to be really sexy in my giving. To me those times were fantastic; to Stan I think at first they were embarrassing and too intense for him to handle. He'd make jokes about them afterwards, about the sweat and the noises and so on, but I could tell he was really uncomfortable about these things. Like I say, he didn't like to give up his control of the marriage bed—he liked to control every aspect of his life really, and every aspect of our lives together. But I wouldn't give way on this—I wanted him to trust me and I wanted to keep our sex life growing. I liked those little tastes of wild give and take and didn't want to give them up. It took a long, long time to break down Stan's barriers—years, really—but we sort of practiced with exercises, with him promising just to let me pet him, and eventually he gave up his need to be in charge and our sex life became very satisfying for both of us.

OPENNESS AND COMMUNICATION

As the California study confirmed, in a sexual relationship based on trust, the partners have little fear—say, of losing the partner, or appearing ridiculous or of failing to arouse the partner—and thus few barriers exist to impede their communication about sex. Open communication about sexual matters is only possible where trust underlies the sexual relationship, and such communication is crucial, for without it partners are unable to shape their sexual life together to their mutual satisfaction. Where no open communication takes place, the sexual life of a couple is likely to assume a certain unchanging character, a pattern based on habit and routine. Only when mates are able to talk freely about sexual matters are enrichment and growth possible. Partners who feel free to discuss all aspects of their sexuality can achieve a range of sexual experience and intimacy undreamed of in their younger years.

Talking Straight

For all the hoopla surrounding the sexual revolution and the permissive society—all the sex pictures, sexy songs, and sexy clothes that bombard us daily—most of us still have a hard time looking our partners in the eye and saying "I like it better when you do this, touching me here, this way," or "How would you like me to touch you? What pleases you? Is this right?" The basic techniques of sexual pleasure are still a taboo subject for a great many people—for some because of ignorance, for others because of a deeply ingrained embarrassment or sense of shame. And a marriage license never worked to extinguish such inhibitions. In fact all too often marriage reinforces them, making all honest talk about sex seem threatening, as if discussion were synonymous with criticism.

Explains Shirley:

> When Burt went to dental school in Chicago, we got married because we didn't want to be separated. I had done some heavy petting, but I had never gone all the way, as we used to say, until we married. Burt had had a couple of affairs. I certainly figured he knew more than I did. For many years he always initiated our lovemaking. It was always nice, but however much we tumbled around, we always ended up with him on top. I kind of felt funny about letting him know that I'd like to end up on top sometimes. I mean, we both liked making love to each other so much I was afraid of messing up a good thing. But finally, after we'd been married for 15 years, when we were making love one time and he tried to turn me on my back, I just said, "Stay where you are, please—just this once." So he did, and really we both found it terribly exciting. It was a new thing for us. When he said how good it was, I told him how I'd hesitated to take the lead away from him for fear he'd see it as a criticism of his lovemaking.

Quite contrary to Shirley's fears, Burt loved it when Shirley took a chance and changed their pattern. Afterward they talked about some of the things that used to feel good but had grown a bit dull. They also loosened up enough to talk about their secret fantasies and giggled over what they now regarded as their shyness in verbalizing their likes and dislikes.

Breaking Through Inhibitions

What is behind the widespread reticence to tell our partners what turns us on? Scan this list and see if any of these common barriers to openness sound familiar.

1. *The fear of seeming "different" or shocking.*

> He: My fantasies are so embarrassing. I get turned on at the sight of sexy underwear, and I'm sure my wife would be shocked at that. I'd love it if she wore that mail-order stuff

once in a while, but I'd never ask her to. She probably wouldn't understand; she'd be so disgusted.

She: I always wanted to make love outside in broad daylight—the idea of being somewhere where someone might see us really excites me. Does that mean I'm perverted? My husband might think so. He's so staid and proper, he'd think I was crazy if I ever suggested it.

2. *The fear of seeming critical.*

He: I love rough loving—I like a little wrestling, struggling, biting—not for pain, but so I can feel a kind of resistance from my partner. I've always been afraid to ask my wife to be more aggressive, though, for fear she'd interpret me as meaning she was too passive. Of course, that's exactly what I would mean! There ought to be a way to say it after 18 years, but I haven't thought of it yet!

She: Sometimes I'd just like my husband to stimulate me with his fingers until I come, without breaking off to have intercourse. He always just stops when he's finished, and then goes to sleep, and I'm left sort of hanging. I always wish I could ask him to stimulate me some more after he's done, but I'm afraid he'll take it to mean I don't like having intercourse with him. I don't want to hurt his feelings or make him mad. I don't even want to wake him up!

3. *Shame at feeling physical pleasure.*

He: My mother once caught me masturbating when I was about eight or nine. She slapped me and yelled that I should never do it again. Ever since I've felt guilty about getting turned on. I'd never ask my wife to do something special just to make me feel good.

She: I really get turned on in the movies. I just love watching those huge, full-color figures on the screen take off their clothes and make love. I've always wanted to go to some X-rated movies with my husband and then make love, but I'd just never ask him. He has no idea of how excited I can get, and I'm glad in a way. Those feelings don't fit with the parts of me he depends on. He'd be shocked and I'd die of shame at my lack of control.

4. *Feelings of futility.*

He: Well, if the spark's not there, it's just not there. We're not going to bring it back by talking about it, that's for sure. It's not worth the trouble of a long drawn-out talk and a possible argument, anyway. I'd do almost anything to avoid an argument, so my first rule is never to talk about sex.

She: My husband's never going to change. So what's the point after all these years of opening up a can of worms like what I want to do in bed? If he doesn't know what I like by now (and, honey, he *doesn't*), what's the sense in trying to explain it? It was his responsibility to find out long ago and he blew it!

5. *The fear of hearing the truth.*

He: I'm afraid if I asked my wife she would make it clear that I don't appeal to her at all, and never have. That's something I've suspected for a long time and I'd just rather not hear it.

She: What if I ask him what would really turn him on and he says a 23-year-old beauty with a condominium and a pool?

6. *The fear of revealing ignorance.*

He: I've always known about women's clitorises and that they were important to their arousal but I've never been sure where Anna's *was*. It just got to be too late to ask after a while. So I never know whether I'm really arousing her clitorally, and, worse, I never know whether she's really satisfied after we make love. After 25 years there's just no way I could admit that I haven't known all along!

She: My husband has always come too quickly for me—*always*, since we first began making love. Whoosh, and it's over. I like to lead up to things gradually, just rubbing and kissing and petting, but for years now I've kept myself from touching him for fear of stimulating him too quickly. Ask him? Well, you know, we're in this pattern now. It'd be hard to ask him what to do to break it.

These barriers to communication can go up early in a relationship and remain indefinitely. Eventually, though, they can threaten the marriage, since trust, not fear, is a hallmark of the well-seasoned marriage.

Sexual Specifics

To establish the trust that a strong marriage needs, partners have to take the very risks they fear. If you are convinced of the need to focus on your sexual life to reach a better level of satisfaction, you will have to risk shocking or criticizing your partner, and risk feeling ashamed or embarrassed upon hearing the truth. How else is it possible to alter the status quo that one or both of you find unacceptable? Together you will have to focus on sexuality and face the issues you have been accustomed to avoiding.

Verbally exploring fantasies, dreams, personal preferences, and secrets—in short, talking straight about sex—can be exciting in itself once you break through the inhibition barriers. Simply talking about your sexuality with your mate could be the first step toward putting the spark back into a flagging sex life. But sometimes the problem is more than shyness or a lack of imagination. Take a look at point 6 on the list: the fear of revealing ignorance. Trust might be the fundamental ingredient in a healthy sexual relationship, but technique based on factual knowledge is necessary too. Where one or both partners have a poor understanding of anatomy and the dynamics of sexual arousal, the couple has very little chance of establishing and maintaining a satisfying sex life over the years. Anna and her husband, though sexually active, were missing the chance for greater sexual satisfaction.

One characteristic of the sexual revolution of the 1960s was a great explosion of knowledge about the physiological aspects of sex, and especially of sexual arousal in women. Before that time a Dark Ages reigned, and people often literally groped around in a hit-or-miss fashion without knowing enough about their own and each other's bodies to maximize their pleasure. If they were unlucky enough never to have a sex partner knowledgeable and uninhibited enough to guide them, they often never learned how to arouse their partners fully or to become fully aroused themselves. It is still never a good idea simply to assume that your partner has an accurate understanding of sexual anatomy—or that you do—especially if you came of age, as most of the subjects in the study did, before accurate information was generally available. Take a lesson from the man and woman quoted in point 6. It is clear they could have profited from doing some reading, looking at some diagrams, asking some questions, and using their eyes and hands on their partners. An hour or two spent simply in gathering information can do wonders to improve one's sexual experience, especially when one has been proceeding on guesswork and misinformation.

The next step, of course, is to exchange information on what arouses you and your partners as individuals, with personal likes and dislikes. Why expect him or her somehow to glean your particular places of pleasure, your favorite movements and levels of pressure, without being told or shown? Let us look at some possible questions you could ask yourselves and each other.

As a woman are your nipples sensitive or perhaps dulled by nursing? Is your clitoris obvious when it becomes erect or does it remain hidden and hard to identify? Are your labia and the inner lining of your vagina sensitive to stimulation or do you prefer a less vaginal approach? Do you like deep or shallow penetration? Is manual or oral arousal to orgasm your choice? Do you like artificial stimulants such as sexy pictures and vibrators? Do you experience orgasms? If so, are they frequent? Are they hard to achieve? Do you have a secret way of reaching them? Are your orgasms light ripples or deep upheavals of pleasure involving the inner recesses of your whole body? If you do not experience orgasms, do you have a suspicion as to how you could? Does oral stimulation arouse you? What could your partner do to help you work on becoming orgasmic? Does self-stimulation play a role in your lovemaking?

As a man **do** you enjoy working up to ejaculation by slow stimulation? Do you respond to light teasing touches or to more vigorous massaging of your penis? Do you prefer that the shaft of your penis be stimulated or just the glans? Is overstimulation a problem? Are your nipples sensitive to sexual stimulation? What other parts of your body are sensitive? If you and your partner arouse each other separately rather than seeking to achieve simultaneous orgasms, would you prefer to come before or after your partner? Does self-stimulation play a role in your lovemaking? Would you like to? For some couples who have been married for years, exploring questions such as these can create a whole new level of intimacy.

Sometimes a third aspect of the self-education process is necessary: learning about sexual dysfunction and how to identify it. Too many people consider themselves seriously and permanently incapable of a healthy sexual response when in fact they are only experiencing, for men, a temporary bout of impotence, natural and predictable in all men, or for women, a lack of understanding of their particular response pattern. Still sexual dysfunction—that is, blockages to a healthy sexual response to stimulation—does exist. However, treatments and techniques for eliminating these conditions exist, too. We live in a time when a full range of treatment is available, from simple manual techniques for treating premature ejaculation to intensive therapy. If you are living in the dark on these matters, read a book, call a friend, find a therapist. But as a first step to turning on the light, talk to each other and get it out in the open!

Settling Old Grudges

Once you break through your inhibitions and begin talking freely about your sex life together, do not be surprised if tempers flare and old resentments surface. Sexuality can become a battle ground in marriage, and unexpressed anger, as in all aspects of interpersonal relations, can dampen sexual passion. Consider this outburst by Tom during a therapy session:

> I've been married to Arlene for 24 years. I'm the president of a bank and at work everyone treats me like I'm important. I am important—at the bank. I meet a lot of attractive women as part of my job. They like and admire me, and so do the men I deal with. But when I come home, how does Arlene greet me? "Take out the garbage, will you, dear, then change the ceiling lightbulbs in the hall. Thanks, darling." That "Thanks, darling" is supposed to make everything all right.

"No thanks, darling" is how Tom felt, both at that moment and later when he and Arlene were in bed together. What does the garbage have to do with making love? Plenty. When we treat each other as though we are important to one another, the stage is set for sexual feelings to emerge. But if all our energy has to go into seeking recognition from our mate, we start to feel like the very garbage we are taking out each night. Tom and Arlene had a lot to talk about once Tom cooled down and was able to express his resentment without bitterness. He stated clearly that he wanted a welcome from Arlene that made him feel she was happy to see him, not a list of things to do. He further explained that when he was upset with her attitude toward him, he lost his sexual desire.

Their talks on the subject taught them that their sexuality was indeed integral to their marriage, not an isolated island of purely physical experience. Once they focused on the questions of mutual respect and trust and really gave attention to their styles of relating to each other outside the bedroom, they were able to refocus on their sexual activity and explore new ways of making love—but not until they had taken care of the unfinished business between them.

Abbie's story makes the same point but comes from the opposite direction:

I'd like to be able to sit down next to Ray on the sofa and watch a TV show to the end—just once. What's so odd about that? But if I sit near him and touch, lean on his shoulder, or hold his hand, he thinks I'm inviting him to make love. Don't get me wrong. Making love is great, but just once I'd like to know how Quincy turns out. I could watch TV by myself, I guess, or sit on the other side of the room, but that's no fun either.

Ray finds Abbie just as attractive now as he did on their wedding day, and she feels the same about him. When Ray was 17, it was not surprising that he thought a girl's sitting next to him and touching him meant he was expected to perform sexually. At 40, though, he ought to know better. Nevertheless in our society men are encouraged to think of most physical contact between men and women as sexual. Traditionally women have been permitted to express physically a wider range of emotions—including the simple affection, separate from desire, that Abbie yearns to express. True, she could take the fact that Ray finds her attractive as a compliment. Many women would. But she is too frustrated at what seems to her to be a lack of subtlety and lack of appreciation for her except on a sexual level. Again, in their discussions of their sex life together, Abbie needed first to broach this subject, a long-repressed complaint, before they could get down to sexual specifics.

Affection

Let us pause in thinking about sex in marriage and acknowledge that most people want and need affectionate expressions, physically and/or verbally. It feels good to be held and cuddled, to hold hands, to wrap your arms around each other without being sexually aroused. Warm and tender embraces and loving gestures are integral to satisfaction in marriage. Maybe some take this for granted, but it is not uncommon for women to complain, "My husband doesn't know anything about touching that doesn't lead to clutching—and bedding." There are men and women who do not enjoy kissing or caressing or who cringe from warm, physical closeness. Some people who enjoy sex are uncomfortable with displays of affection. Often they are struggling with the residue of earlier experiences and have problems with intimacy. Some men and women can gradually get over their discomfort by gentle approaches by their mates; others will find that professional help is useful, and still others simply accept a marriage that does not include this ingredient.

Making Changes

Talking about sex can be exciting and encouraging for marriage partners, but in the effort to change or revitalize their sex life, at some point a couple needs to experiment actively. One basic way of breaking a predictable routine is literally to change the place and time of your lovemaking. With a little creativity and imagination, a couple can find new places in which to make love whose very newness will enhance the eroticism of their sex play. A couple preoccupied with young children, for instance, can boost their sex life simply by turning the kids over to a sitter for a night and retreating to a hotel. Another couple might choose a motel with a water bed and X-rated movies on a closed-circuit television. Here is Pam's view.

> When things get hairy around here, I arrange for the kids to sleep at a friend's house. Then Harvey and I can be children and play with each other without fear of interruption or intrusion. That doesn't mean we never make love when the kids are home, but it's really special when Harvey and I are here totally alone in the house together.

Millie, who has been married to Irv for 23 years, found another way.

> When two of the kids had gone to college, we sold our big house and moved into a condominium. We had a bedroom for Lisa to use when she came home on weekends, but it was kind of small, so to make it look bigger, I had one whole wall lined with mirrors. Irv and I discovered that making love in that room was a whole new thing. And no visitor ever says with a snicker, "I see you have mirrors in your bedroom." They don't even think about it, since the mirrors are in Lisa's room.

For more ideas on how to break old habits and deepen sexual experiences, see the "Exercises."

THE WHOLE VIEW

Let us remind ourselves to keep things in perspective.

Focusing solely on sex as a panacea to difficulties in a marriage is a big mistake. Sex is not identical with love, **nor** is sex the sole measure of the quality of a marriage. People can and do love each other deeply, and can and do have strong and enduring marriages, while **experiencing** sexual difficulties. It is important to remember that the California study showed sexual satisfaction most of the time, not all the time, to be characteristic of successful long-term marriages. In a healthy long-term marriage other factors assume equal importance as time goes on, and the partners take pleasure in the deepening of the relationship and its increasing complexity on many levels, not just the sexual ones. Ideally the couple's sex life is intrinsic to their relationship as a whole, and grows and changes without obsessive concern. Like any other area, it needs attention at times, but sex should be seen as the reflector of the overall quality of the marriage, not its sole determinant. For a sense of how sexuality is integrated into a successful long-term marriage, read what Bob has to say about making love with his wife of 20 years.

Marsha and I have been making love together for a long time. At first it was incredibly exciting just being together, and I thought that was perfection. But I realized recently that as the years have gone by, sex between us has become better and better. See this pipe I'm smoking? I think of our lovemaking as ripening during our marriage the way this meerschaum has. We may not have the same bite and sharpness we had at the beginning, but there's a richness, a mellowness, a depth to our satisfaction that just wasn't there when we first started out.

EXERCISES

The following exercises are designed to help you and your mate understand your sexual feelings and needs, and to offer you some tools to enrich your sex lives.

1. Answer the following questions and ask your mate to do the same. Compare your answers and talk about them. Use this as an opportunity to share your feelings and to learn more about what pleases you, and what might even please you more. The sexual repertoire benefits from freedom between both of you.

a). I feel we make love often enough
   most of the time ___ some of the time ___ rarely ___

b). I feel you are satisfied with our lovemaking
   most of the time ___ some of the time ___ rarely ___

c). Our sex life is exciting to me
   most of the time ___ some of the time ___ rarely ___

d). I have orgasms/I can time my orgasms well
   most of the time ___ some of the time ___ rarely ___

e). I know when you have orgasms/the timing of your orgasms is good
   most of the time ___ some of the time ___ rarely ___

f). When I don't have an orgasm/When I come too soon or not at all, I feel embarrassed to let you know
   most of the time ___ some of the time ___ rarely ___

g). We spend enough time in foreplay before actually having intercourse
   most of the time ___ some of the time ___ rarely ___

h). I hesitate to suggest something new in bed
   most of the time ___ some of the time ___ rarely ___

i). I would like to be more innovative and creative in bed
   most of the time ___ some of the time ___ rarely ___

j). I have fun in bed
   most of the time ___ some of the time ___ rarely ___

k). I worry about losing my erection/my clitoral sensitivity
   most of the time ___ some of the time ___ rarely ___

l). When we have been openly affectionate I feel more sexual
   most of the time ___ some of the time ___ rarely ___

m). It's easier to make love when _____
   _____

n). It's especially arousing to me when you _____
   _____

o). I don't enjoy sex with you when you _____
   _____

p). I enjoy making love most when _____
   _____

q). If I feel aroused, and you do something that makes me angry, I can't respond to you:
   most of the time ___ some of the time ___ rarely ___

r). Upsetting things in my life outside our relationship can interfere with my sexual desire:
   most of the time ___ some of the time ___ rarely ___

s). When I don't have an orgasm during intercourse and you do, I find it difficult to ask you to continue to stimulate me until I climax.

yes __, no __, sometimes __.

t). I feel free to try anything sexual with you that I want to, as long as it's okay with you.

yes __, no __, sometimes __.

u). I find it easy to say no to sexual activities that feel uncomfortable to me.

yes __, no __, sometimes __.

v). I envy the variety of sexual relationships that single people enjoy

most of the time __, some of the time __, rarely __.

2. Make your own lists of personal preferences and questions about your partner's preferences using the foregoing questions as models. Ask your spouse to do the same and exchange lists as a prelude to talking.

3. Caress each other's bodies without trying to arouse each other sexually. That is, stroke each other in turn, touching all parts of the body except the genitals. Ask your mate to tell you what feels particularly good and linger there. The purpose is simply to give pleasure to your partner without progressing toward intercourse and to learn what pleases him or her in particular.

4. The next time you make love, let the partner who does not usually initiate the sexual encounter do so, just to see how it feels. For partners who have difficulty making the first move, try initiating a playing time together—perhaps by inviting your mate to take a shower or a nude swim with you.

5. Tell each other a fantasy you have had about making love. If the fantasy can be acted out, do it together. Perhaps you cannot do it on a South Pacific shore, but you can try a swimming pool, or even a bathtub.

6. When you're making love next time and you feel a desire for your partner to do something harder or softer, faster or slower, more vigorously or more gently, make a point of saying so or of conveying the message explicitly by using your hands and your body.

Above all, lighten up! Have fun! After you've read this chapter and done the exercises, toss the book off the bed and enjoy yourselves!

5

MARRIAGE AND INFIDELITY

Conspicuously absent from the preceding chapter on revitalizing one's sex life within marriage was any reference to the option many people consider first, if only in their imaginations. That option, of course, is extramarital sex—a blanket term (excuse the pun) that covers everything from quick one-nighters to extended, emotionally entangling love affairs, to excursions couples take together into the world of mate swapping and group sex.

Anyone who, from the relative safety of even the shakiest marriage, has considered having a sexual episode outside marriage knows how quickly such thoughts can lead to unanswerable questions. Chief among them is: Will the marriage survive if I do this? Few can answer this question with confidence, let alone accuracy. Typically, excitement, self-deceit, and, as I've noted often before, society's untrue and frequently destructive sex myths combine to cloud our thinking when we turn the "should I/shouldn't I" question over and over in our minds.

What can the well-seasoned marriage teach us about the effects of extramarital sex? All spouses being human, all having no doubt stood at one time or another on the brink of the unknown, all have wondered whether or not to plunge into an extramarital affair. Partners in most successful long-term marriages that I have observed, both in the study population and in my clinical practice, have *tried* to maintain their commitment to the principles of monogamy—sexual fidelity and honesty regarding sexual matters. Where one mate or another has transgressed, either with a single affair or a series of them, the effect on the marriage was neither positive nor constructive. In rare instances the effect is neutral; in a very few the marriage not only recovers, but may even be strengthened. But in general the argument that one spouse's extramarital episode will be "good for the marriage" is pure rationalization and, in the short and long run, not helpful. If preservation of the marriage were the only goal, then it might make sense to "fill in" with affairs once in a while, but for people who want deeply satisfying, warm, trustful relationships, these sexual excursions take something away from the overall quality of the marriage.

This said, exploring the interrelated topics of monogomy and extramarital sex can be fruitful in many ways. Above all it can help us to clear away the myths, fears, and self-deceits that often muddy our thinking on these subjects and to clarify our understanding of marriage and its meaning for our lives.

THE "BURDEN" OF MONOGAMY

"It's unnatural for men to be monogamous," argues Jack, 38, who is feeling shackled by the promise of fidelity he has kept during his 18-year marriage.

> There are so many tempting-looking women around, and I assume women feel similarly tempted by the men they see. Why should we all have to force ourselves to stay away from each other just because we're married—especially since, let's face it, after 18 years things are bound to get a little old in bed?

One answer to Jack's question can be found in the preceding chapter. At the basis of all successful long-term marriages is a major necessary ingredient: trust. Trust is an abstract notion. We have explored its specific meanings in a number of particular circumstances already. In the context of this chapter, trust means the belief in one's partner's strong commitment to the principles of monogamous marriage built upon experience supportive of this belief system.

Unless you are married to a psychopathic liar, you are likely to know whether your mate is being truthful to you. There will be inconsistencies and embarrassment to alert you to deceit. He never tells you where he stays on business trips, she does not inform you of delays at the office, he is dishonest in dealing with other family members, she lives a life of one cover-up after another. It may take years to discover the "secret life" of a mate, with its layers of fabrications, but eventually the truth emerges, often with disastrous results.

In one case a man managed to have continual affairs with women over a 12-year period while being sexually active with his wife. There were no clues, and although certain mutual friends knew of his infidelity, they never shared this knowledge with his wife. In his case his "innocent" affairs led to dissatisfaction with his marriage, and finally a divorce. When his wife learned of his multiple affairs with other women, she had trouble understanding them, since their sex life had always been great together. Only later she saw that her husband wanted a totally different kind of life-style, which he sought in his sexual escapades. He felt a great desire to bring sexual pleasure to as many women as he could, since he so often felt he failed to bring any other kind of pleasure to his wife or to other women. His complicated needs and his inability to be honest with his wife conspired for years to thwart his marriage. This is not the usual experience. Most often there are ample clues to what is really going on with only one's own denial of reality blurring one's vision. For those who do not want to know what is happening, there are plenty of ways to avoid the bad news.

Some people may interpret monogamy to mean that sexual infidelity is altogether excluded while others stretch the definition to allow for a greater or lesser degree of extramarital sex. Here is where the fundamental need for open communication comes in. Does your mate believe that marriage requires strict sexual fidelity? Do you? Does he or she perceive situations in which exceptions might apply to the strict-fidelity commitment? Do you? No matter how long you have been married or how certain you are about your mate's acceptance of the marriage vows, without openly communicating on the subject you and your mate may be operating under different definitions and "rules" of monogamy.

John and Barbara's story illustrates how clashing definitions of monogamy and its obligations can cause problems.

The two married when John entered medical school and had a rough go of it financially for a long while. Life did not begin to seem worry-free until John landed a well-paying position at a prestigious metropolitan hospital. The two bought a house in the suburbs, and for the first time in many years, Barbara was able to quit working. She had time on her hands and anxiety on her mind, for she was well aware that John spent his long workday among many intelligent and vibrant female colleagues, nurses, nurse's aids, and other female hospital personnel. Here is Barbara's story.

> Well, I know that I'd succumb to temptation in those circumstances. I mean, there was a distance between us every day; lots of times John would stay on in the city when he was too tired or busy to come home. I just started assuming he was, well, doing what I'd do, the lucky stiff, taking his pick of the available staff and generally having a high old time. After all, he's a very attractive guy. I began believing it so strongly I walked around mad all the time, looking for a way to get even. I started seeing a way in the eyes of our gardener, who seemed to be around, working on the rock garden or clipping the hedges, whenever I was lying by the pool. It wasn't long before we were having a furiously passionate affair, and not long after it started, John walked in on us in bed. He went crazy with anger, but when I accused him of fooling around at the hospital and told him I was only getting even, he was stunned. He couldn't say anything but "Never! I'd *never* do such a thing. I've never even considered being unfaithful to you, never!" Well, it was just a case of crossed wires, I guess, a costly misunderstanding. And we never got over it. That was the end of our marriage.

Such is the fate of "trust" within marriage if it is not anchored solidly in a clear and mutual understanding. John and Barbara may well have avoided the event that was fatal to their marriage if Barbara had not projected her feelings onto John, but had expressed her fears to her husband and clarified their committment to monogamy.

Agreeing in Principle

Still, talking and doing are two different things, a lesson we all apparently have to learn a million times in a million ways. Many couples, after discussing the issue of fidelity as freely and fully as possible, come to the conclusion that it is indeed an impossible burden over a decades-long marriage. A frequent refrain sung by both men and women is that sexual involvement with people outside the marriage can be revitalizing for the marital sexual relationship. The stimulation, the experience, and above all the reaffirmation of the infidel's sexual attractiveness can draw the other into the game and reignite the old spark like nothing else—or so the argument goes.

A popular book, *Open Marriage*, enlarges on this premise by asserting that partners who respect each other's individuality and who maintain a properly mature attitude may get to a level of maturity where they can accept extramarital activity on their mates' part (though the authors imply that they themselves have not attained such a level). Again it all sounds good on paper, or in a rambling after-dinner talk with good friends around the table. But even the authors of *Open Marriage* note the potential difficulty of couples successfully maintaining their own relationship while having lovers on the side. During the course of my practice, I have seen marriages recover from extramarital episodes but not thrive on account of them.

Why not? What comes between the theory and the experience to spell difficulty, if not disaster, for the extra marital explorer and his or her mate? Are we still so bound by Old Testament morality that "Thou shalt not commit adultery" makes us quake and trip on our own windy intentions? Or is it simply old-fashioned jealousy and possessiveness?

Sex and Emotions

In my experience the answer lies not in simple envy nor in formal morality, but in the dynamics of human interaction. The chief danger for a married person pursuing a "casual" affair is becoming involved emotionally with the outside lover. Too often the adventure that might have been intended to reenergize the adulterer—and, in his or her mind, the marriage—only serves to widen the rift between the original partners by involving the wanderer in an intense, bewildering, and utterly distracting emotional entanglement. Susan relates the following incident:

> I walked into his house barely breathing, my heartbeat making a din in my head. I was about to find out how it would feel to be with another man, something I'd been imagining for years. I'd been attracted to Eric for months but never dared to take

him up on his flirtations until one night when Harvey was away on business and the children were away at camp. The time just seemed to be right. It was all so easy. It felt innocent enough to me. I planned to have a great time for a night and then walk away from the whole thing. Little did I know that I'd fall desperately, helplessly in love.

Susan found herself caught with more than her sexual feelings aroused. Her "one-nighter" developed into a continuing affair that caused a major upheaval from which her marriage never recovered. Prior to this affair, Susan and Harvey had been feeling somewhat bored with each other. Both were working and they rarely saw each other. At 41 and 38, respectively, they had lost the excitement that had spurred their young marriage 20 years earlier. They felt connected to each other, but failed to make a constructive attempt to confront their boredom and do something about it together. Susan's adventure diverted her from seeking a solution with her husband. The disruption of a full-blown love affair was too great a strain for the marriage and the two divorced. The affair with Eric, too, collapsed under the emotional stress, and Susan was left wondering how it had all happened and whether the turmoil had been worthwhile.

An interesting but predictable finding of the California study was that women are far more likely than men to equate sexual involvement with emotional involvement and to experience both together. Another way of expressing this finding is to say that women are far less likely than men to pursue and enjoy sexual encounters without feeling some affection for the lover. Many possible explanations exist for this male–female discrepancy, and the phenomenon has many ramifications, generally problematical, in the sexual area of interpersonal relations. One such ramification is the frequency with which women become involved, as Susan did, even when they intend to enjoy a casual, purely .physical affair and walk away emotionally untouched.

Consider Greg's smug remarks about his wife Carole on this matter.

Really, I don't care if Carole has sex with another man, at least not so far as the sex itself is concerned. But the problem is that, well, I just know my wife would probably get hung up on the guy. My little affairs don't really touch me emotionally. I don't love the women I go to bed with on the side. I love only Carole. But I don't think it could be the same for her.

The women's movement has shown concern over this discrepancy and has argued that truly liberated women can and should have the same attitude toward "casual sex"—that is, recreational sex—as men. I wonder if this is either possible or desirable. Traditionally dads nationwide have been winking at their teenage sons and urging them to "Have a good time, son, but don't get into trouble," while neither they nor their wives say any such thing to their daughters. I would argue that instead of urging women to sever sex from affection and to go to bed solely for the physical pleasure of it, the women's movement should work to change the traditional upbringing of boys, educating parents to teach both boys and girls that sex and emotion are inextricably linked and that a full experience of sexuality involves both aspects.

This is not to say that for men sexuality is always, or even often, devoid of emotion. Consider Dick's remarks:

> Of course I've thought of having an affair. I've thought about it lots of times, expecially in the days when Frances hardly ever wanted to make love. We had three kids within five years, and I was working such long hours in my pharmacy that I couldn't give Frances much of a hand at home. But no matter how long my day had been, I was ready for some love when I got home. Not Frances. By the time she got those babies into bed, all she wanted to do was sleep. So you know, I used to imagine going to bed with this one or that one. Only I never did because just having sex with someone didn't really appeal to me. And then, of course, the kids got older and we got older too, and we talked more, and Frances had her tubes tied and didn't worry any more about getting pregnant. Everything changed. There's enough sex in our house these days to satisfy Don Juan himself.

Dick did indeed fantasize about recreational sex, as many people of both sexes do who nevertheless actually opt for sex with an emotional component. For him his imaginary excursions were enough to satisfy his urge.

For Joel, however, fantasy was not enough, yet his remarks show that he saw a clear distinction between recreational sex and sex that is linked to affection. He took measures to protect himself from becoming emotionally involved with women other than his wife.

> I always picked women who were safe. They were usually nothing much to look at, and quite a bit older than me. I couldn't imagine that any one of them would ever pose any kind of threat to my relationship with Rita.

Another example of a husband restraining himself from becoming emotionally involved is Herb, who discusses the differences between his extramarital sex life and sex with his long-time wife, Monica.

> I would say that Monica and I are sexually pretty active. We've been married for 25 years and we still make love two or three times a week. I still find Monica very exciting and she feels the same about me. But I like variety. We married young, and I missed all that fooling around guys usually do before they get married. I'm a lawyer, and I meet a lot of really gorgeous, interesting women all the time, and when I can, I go to bed with them. I think just doing the same thing all the time is boring. I can have sex with someone without getting emotionally involved. I guess I do feel guilty sometimes though, and I'm not so free with these young chicks as I am with Monica. It's really better with Monica than with anyone else. Most of the men I know have divorced their wives and married girls in their 20s. I don't want to miss out. I kind of like that swinging life-style, but I don't want a divorce. There's something good between Monica and me. I've seen plenty of divorces, and there isn't one without a hassle over money, or kids, or both. Who needs it? So I have these affairs and it works out fine.

In reality it was not so fine. This marriage ended in divorce three years later when his wife became aware of his other life. Lest I seem to be implying that married women are incapable of having recreational sex, let us end this section with a quote from Rosa, who had a string of casual lovers throughout the last years of her marriage.

> I just decided to do it one day with the UPS man at work. We'd been eyeing each other for more than a year, and one day when he was making a delivery, he asked me out to lunch. That's the way to handle it, I found out—at lunch. I didn't even have to lie to George. I'd work in the city, have my little lunch-hour fling with whoever it was at the time, and then somehow it would all be behind me at five o'clock. I'd get on the bus and go home to the suburbs and do that life. About a year or two after that first fling with Mr. UPS, I started making dates at night occasionally, and that was a lot harder to get used to because I'd have to lie to pull it off. I invented some real doozies, and it was exciting somehow to have George think I was at the town council meeting while I was really in another world, in a bar or a motel room. It was too exciting in a way, because George and I just quit making love altogether. Then one day he found out that I hadn't been where I'd said I was and the whole thing came tumbling down. That was it for the marriage. He left that night and never came back.

George and Rosa's stories open up a can of worms that is unavoidable in a discussion of marital infidelity: deceit.

LYING

Here is Bob's story of what happened to him.

It's been three years, and I still think of lies that Lisa told me that I hadn't thought of before, and each one does me in. I know it's easy to say, but I honestly believe I could have handled the fact that she was having an affair if it hadn't been for the lying. It's funny, after I found out about the affair she never really understood why I couldn't just forgive and forget. But for our whole marriage, 21 years, I never once worried that she wasn't telling me the truth about anything. That had always been our thing—how direct and open we were. Then I found out she'd been spinning tales every day about where she'd been, what she'd been doing, and, well, like I say, it's been three years and we've been divorced for two and I'm still not over it. I feel like such a fool.

Here we have a pretty broad clue as to why the effects of sexual infidelity are negative for most marriages. Infidelity usually involves deceit, and deceit, pure and simple, is a betrayal of trust. With trust identified as a crucial component in all successful long-term marriages, is it any wonder that deceit can wreak havoc on a marital relationship? It is the lying, not the partner's intimacy with another, that many find impossible to forgive.

Modern Marriages of Convenience

At the same time, in the course of discussions about extramarital sex one frequently hears such comments as, "I don't care if my husband has an affair as long as I don't know about it." One woman I treated took this attitude a step further: "Why did he have to confess to me? Why couldn't he have carried his guilt around without dragging me through the mill? Now he's waiting around like a whipped puppy for me to absolve him, and that's what I'll have to do if I want to stay married."

My question here is this: In light of the importance of trust to a marriage, is it really viable to choose "not to know"? Isn't such a choice simply trading quality for security, a settling for poor-quality merchandise in order to get anything at all?

The classical marriage of convenience—in which a woman married as a means of ensuring her livelihood—began to go out with World War II, when women entered the work force in substantial numbers and gained the wherewithal to exist financially on their own. However, more subtle forms of marriages of convenience currently exist on both sides: among women who stay married long after they cease to experience satisfaction or pleasure so they can live the life-styles their husbands' incomes make possible; among men who stay married long after warmth for their mates has died in order to be known as "family men"; and among countless people of both sexes who feel too frightened at the prospect of being on their own to leave an empty marriage.

Many people involved in such modern marriages of convenience pursue extramarital affairs as a way of feeling good again, even if only for an afternoon or evening. Although there are moments in most marriages when one of the mates feels like being in the arms of some other person, either because of a temporary rift or owing to a strong chemical attraction, in most healthy marriages both partners feel enough warmth for and contentment with their mates to resist the urge to act out sexually. Where a continuing urge to be with someone else exists, the quality of the relationship is usually so poor that the value of the marriage itself is—or should be—called into question.

After all, some marriages may not be worth saving. Often the cost to one's self-esteem of staying in a marriage of poor quality is greater than the turmoil of divorce and subsequent new lease on life. The idea is not to save all marriages from divorce at all costs. Rather one must learn to assess one's marriage in terms of what has to be done to improve its quality. Further, one has to decide whether what needs to be done can be done, or whether terminating the marriage is the wisest choice. Consider Marie's description of the last four years of her marriage to Paul.

> I knew and yet I didn't know. I mean, I knew something was going on but I didn't know he was seeing other women. I wasn't really surprised when I found out, though. I'll never know why he didn't just ask me for a divorce in the first

place—he just couldn't admit that he wanted to leave me and the kids, I guess. So he dragged us through four years of silence, temper tantrums where he went slamming out of the house, and months at a time of moodiness and meanness, trying to get me to throw him out. A couple of times I found things around that had to have been from other women—a note, a hotel key—but I was so dense I didn't figure it out. No, that's not it. I didn't want to figure it out, didn't want to know. If I admitted to myself that he was seeing someone else, I would have had to leave him, but I was petrified of being on my own. I got married when I was 19 years old, and before that my father took care of me. The idea of running the house on my own, and of getting a job and the rest of it, scared me so much I chose not to see what he was pushing at my face. Now I realize that he was scared too. Otherwise why didn't he just leave me? Well, he did finally, of course, but only after he'd given me clues a three-year-old would pick up. He came home one night just reeking of perfume. I had to notice it, and had to ask him. That was the way he finally got me to see he wanted to leave us. It would have saved us all a lot of time and pain—about four years' worth—if he'd just come out with it in the first place.

The moral of Marie's story is not hard to see: read the signals and find out what they mean. More often than not in a marriage, the handwriting on the wall is a message from your mate. The hard part is not reading it, but interpreting its meaning and doing something about it.

STRESS: A COMMON CULPRIT

The message on the wall that one's mate is involved in extramarital sex does not always mean that the unfaithful partner wants out. Often, however, it does indicate that he or she is experiencing stress of one sort or another and is seeking solace, or diversion, outside the home. Chester reveals that this was true of him when his business started plummeting.

Jan and I have had a very good marriage though she has always been more conservative than I. I never cheated on her, never went out with any women after we married, and as a matter of fact never considered fidelity such a big deal, because I never wanted to go out with anyone else. But last year when the business began to go into a tailspin, I panicked. I met a good-looking woman on a business trip, and for the first time in 22 years I became involved. After that it was an exciting adventure. We met in the middle of the day or early in the evening. It felt so good to be playing hooky from my business and all that bad news. I just couldn't hack sitting at my desk waiting for the telephone to ring. The excitement, the sex, made me forget all that. My wife was never suspicious since she had never had any reason to worry about affairs and she knew the business was in trouble, so my "working late" didn't concern her. I knew, of course, that I didn't mean very much to the other woman—I always had the feeling I could break it off any time and she'd just smile and say good-bye. I loved it, though, and never considered giving it up. But the balloon burst one day when my wife happened to call the office when I was supposed to be there. Once that happened the affair was over, and Jan and I have been trying to get over the whole thing ever since.

For Chester and Jan psychotherapy was essential to efforts at recovery. It involved extensive reassessment of their ways of relating to each other. Further, both had to learn how much the ups and downs of Chester's business meant to their relationship. Jan had to learn how to express her support and concern when business went poorly, and Chester had to come to grips with conditions as they were, without fleeing headlong into sexual distractions. He had to learn that his way of coping with stress jeopardized the marriage he in fact cared about deeply and wanted to preserve.

These two were lucky. They were able to weather a period of intense stress, exacerbated many times by Chester's affair, and to assess the meaning of the signals they had misread over the years. When the hurt and anger had subsided somewhat, both partners were able to recognize that Chester's affair was the symptom of a deeper distress, and both affirmed that the marriage was worth saving despite the breach of trust they had experienced. In this sense some might see Chester's infidelity resulting in a strengthening of the bond between the spouses, a bond so strong that it survived difficulties that would have destroyed a less secure relationship. It is more likely that their marriage survived in spite of the affair, not because of it. A marriage that does not survive such difficulties is not necessarily one without value, but one that has been too damaged to continue.

AGREED-ON ADVENTURES

Two scenarios remain to be explored: encounters involving both partners and temporary separations. Both might be considered compromise solutions arrived at when one or both marriage partners wants to experience extramarital sex while maintaining the marriage. The first involves mutual excursions into extramarital sex. This is Gail's story.

We met Carrie and Stu at Arthur's boss's house. They were so lively and exciting we invited them to a barbecue the next weekend. We were actually a little surprised when they accepted our invitation; they seemed a bit too sophisticated for us. But we began to see quite a bit of them. One evening Stu suggested that it might be fun if we all found out how each of us made love, and that maybe we ought to try a swap. At first Arthur and I thought he was kidding, but then several times Carrie talked about playing switch, and finally we just decided to do it. Since we all agreed, I couldn't really see anything wrong with it, and at first Arthur and I were amazed at how exciting it was. We came back from our encounters with Carrie and Stu and told each other all about it. Somehow, far from interfering with our wanting each other, it seemed to make our own sex life just that much more exciting. But it was different for them. They were fighting a lot and it got so they didn't want to sleep with each other at all. When we were all together, their bad feelings about each other started to come out, and they tried to involve us in that too. So Arthur and I just stopped. We don't see them anymore at all. They weren't doing it just for fun—swapping was serious business for them.

The fact that Gail and Arthur agreed to the switches made the sex play a mutual adventure rather than a breach of trust. They avoided the lying and guilt associated with most affairs, though they did risk the possibility one or the other might have become emotionally involved with the new partner, or one might have wanted to continue the encounters after the other wanted to stop. Any conflict Gail and Arthur might have experienced around the swaps would have raised the age-old question: "Is it worth risking the marriage?" Most couples who have been involved in these kinds of arrangements have found them unsettling to the marriage.

Another circumstance under which this question might echo even more ominously is the agreed-on temporary separation. An individual who feels that monogamy has become a burden too heavy to bear forever may well propose that he or she go off for a while to live singly while remaining legally married and intending to return. The partner of such a person who is similarly unwilling to end the marriage, not recognizing other options, might accept such a plan. Here again, if both partners agree that the promise of fidelity is to be temporarily nullified, whatever sexual activity takes place might be viewed as fair play rather than as a breach of trust or an attack on the marriage bond. Here is Stella's account of her temporary separation from David:

> I married David when I was 20. I never had had sex with anyone but him. I was pretty happy with our sex life, but wondered sometimes what sex would be like with someone else. There were a lot of ways in which David was really getting to me. It seemed to me nothing I did was good enough for him. When I was about 36 and the kids were in their teens, I thought they were old enough to withstand a divorce. I'd thought about it for a long time, but never brought it up until then. Dave really didn't know how unhappy I'd been and when I said "divorce" he got scared. He wanted to go for counseling. The therapist made him see that I was feeling I'd missed out because I hadn't had a chance to live on my own before I got married. I didn't want any more therapy; I really didn't want to save my marriage. So we agreed on a separation. We decided we could both date and live our own lives but not think about divorcing yet. Two months with other men was enough. After that I couldn't wait to get back home and back into therapy. It turned out to be great. Dave was a lot more sensitive to my feelings and we really came to a new understanding. And I felt I'd seen the big bad world—enough of it to last me forever.

Stella simply had to leave and act out her fantasies. Only when she had confronted reality and had been disappointed was she able to return to the marriage and work on its problems without feeling deprived. The risk, of course, was that Stella might have loved being on her own, or that David might have, much to his surprise, or that one or the other might have become emotionally involved with a third person during their separation. We all know of many "temporary" separations that become permanent and that in retrospect seem merely the second to last step toward divorce. But for married people who are unsure of what their cravings mean, or who are willing to keep their options open without ending the marriage outright, a temporary separation can be a viable, if risky, course of action.

MIDLIFE: IMPACT ON MARRIAGE

Midlife, with its opportunities for trying new things, can send shock waves through traditional relationships. On the positive side, it can be a time for career shifts, or a time to earn that B.A., M.A., or Ph.D. that earlier eluded one. Women who generously volunteered themselves to PTA's, hospitals, and charities may now seek paid employment. Men who decide that this quest for prestige or security is no longer necessary may want to cut back their working hours, or even retire. Some people totally change their ways of life in order to pursue new dreams.

On the negative side, this midlife period, characterized to a greater or lesser degree by feelings of pressure to "live" while there's still time, can be devastating to careers and can cause marital relationships to take a nosedive. Some marriages dissolve after 25 to 30 years from the effects of midlife fears. Other couples may have been struggling through the years, waiting for things to get better, their marriages maintaining themselves out of economic necessity, for the "sake of the children," for health reasons, for the image and the comfort of regular sexual partners. Now in midlife these couples may realize things are not going to get better. They may see this time of life as a last chance to grab for happiness. Though change in itself is not bad, it is always disruptive to the equilibrium of a relationship. When one marriage partner is pleased with the status quo but the other is not, change can be particularly frightening and resisted fiercely.

Some Like It Young

If a marriage ends with the husband or wife linking up with a much younger person, it may mean a last try at youth for that partner, or it may be a true reflection of his or her current needs. Many armchair therapists jump too quickly to what seem to be obvious conclusions. Some of those conclusions are dead wrong. Linda explains it this way:

Mark just would never consider living the life-style that appealed to me, and all through the years I kept telling him how unhappy I was. When David, our youngest, left for Berkeley, I told Mark I was through. I didn't want a therapist to "save" our marriage. I wanted out. I involved myself in all kinds of hiking and sports activities, met a terrific man, nine years younger than I, and we're having a great time together. I know lots of people think I'm terrible, but they just don't understand how awful it was, living in a way that was just miserable for me. With the children gone, I figured this is it, either change it now or forget it—so I changed it.

Linda wanted changes in which her husband had no desire to participate. She chose to try to get what she wanted. She met a man who happened to be younger and with whom she shared a wide array of interests. Chances are good that this relationship could develop into a lasting one as long as the young man does not want children. Is Linda trying to recapture her youth, or just trying to enjoy her middle age?

Change: Fun for Some, Hurtful for Others

The men and women who lose their marital partners to divorce or death are tossed into a tough, highly competitive arena. Women over 50 often find that they are considered less desirable than their male counterparts. It is okay for men to have lines on their faces or gray hair, but women must remain eternally youthful to be invited into the game.

When marriages dissolve there are dramatic shifts in life-style from coupledome to singleness, from a sense of security to a bewildering sense of aloneness. Depression, anxiety, and physical complaints can come to the fore until a balance is achieved. Some people try to solve the problem by joining new interest groups, taking classes, trying activities geared for the single person. These can be helpful, but they cannot fill the emptiness one feels at being cast out from the married world. It is never easy to cope with loss, and in the case of divorce, complicated feelings are aroused that touch on one's whole sense of worth.

These feelings of abandonment, rejection, and helplessness distort one's view of one's self and require reparative work. Expressing anger, grieving over both the lost love (like grieving over death) and over the part of you that feels empty, readies you, in time, to get on with living. It can mean starting a new career, making a career shift, developing new relationships with people who have time to share activities, ideas, and feelings. Some people get a boost by joining support groups where their feelings are understood, and where there is a sense of camaraderie. Misery really does like company; then it does not feel so miserable.

It is a blow to the ego when a woman finds her husband has left her for a younger woman or a man finds his wife has left him for a younger man. Besides their own consciousness that they are getting older, they feel faced with further evidence of their diminishing charms. Many women suffer extreme loss of self-confidence when their husbands hook up with much younger women. They should ask themselves, "Was the marriage feeling good, was lovemaking still a priority, did I try to stay abreast of changes in my mate?" And then ask, "Was my mate more vulnerable to attention by others because of things going on inside him or her or because of our relationship?" If your answer is the latter, you can learn for the future to pay attention to your relationship. If your answer is the former, you will realize that you cannot control what goes on inside another person. A man or woman can be a ripe target for the flattery and excitement of a new relationship.

There are people who do better with beginnings than they do in sustaining a relationship. Not all people are good candidates for long-term marriages. Those who want to remain in a satisfying marriage know that continuing attention is necessary throughout the relationship.

CONCLUSIONS

Let us go full circle by restating that extramarital sexual activity rarely does a marriage any good. It is true that some marriage bonds survive the upheaval that an outside affair can cause, and may even be strengthened as a result of the healing process. But such strengthening usually occurs in spite of the infidelity, not because of it.

The California study and other research confirm this conclusion. It is a logical one when we examine the basis of a healthy marriage. Most infidelity involves deceit and deceit cracks that foundation of a healthy marriage: trust. A broken trust is a broken marriage, and only rarely does a couple recover from such a fundamental assault on the bond between them.

In a few instances extramarital activity involves no deceit: that to which both partners agree or that which occurs during a temporary separation. But this too involves risk and can bring with it that age-old question that everyone who considers extramarital sex must eventually ask: "Is it worth risking my marriage for?"

EXERCISES

The following questions are designed to stimulate your examination of this potentially hazardous area in your married life.

1. Ask yourself whether an involvement sexually with another person is worth the possible damage to your marriage. If the answer is no, talk to your mate about your unhappiness with the marriage.

2. If you are currently involved in extramarital affairs, ask yourself if the pleasure you gain there is unobtainable at home. Could another avenue of exploration enliven your sex life at home without including other partners?

3. Do you feel you are missing the "action" of younger, more sexually experienced women or men and therefore want a "taste" of it before it is too late? If you do, are there other ways to add new spice to your life with your current mate?

4. Do you feel that recreational sex is equally available to you and your mate? Are you and your mate playing by the same rules? If not, try discussing what you want with your mate so as not to violate the trust between you.

6

LEARNING TO ARGUE—
THE RIGHT WAY

I JUST COULDN'T TAKE THE constant battle. It wore me out, I wasn't used to it. Carping, picking, throwing little innuendoes around—Adrian and I were always at each other, and I thought it was just going to wear us out. I wondered if that was marriage, the continual barrage of discontent and aggravation. If that was to be our lot for the rest of our lives together, I wanted to bail out—no kidding. I just couldn't face 20, 30, 40 years of that kind of constant aggravation and tension.

So complained Michael, a lawyer married for 16 years to Adrian, an editor. He was right. The future he painted for himself and his wife was pretty grim, but it is by no means an uncommon fate. Let us have Adrian's version to round out the picture.

I knew Michael hated confrontations with me, but I couldn't hold back when something was bothering me. My family was always fighting but we never thought of it as something terrible; it was just our way of working out disagreements. I mean, there are always going to be disagreements when people live together, right? But I couldn't ever get him to argue with me and work it out; he just clammed up. So I guess I got my jabs and punches in whenever I could. Carp? Well, maybe, but how else could I get things out if he ducked out of every confrontation? He saw it as me picking at him all the time and complaining and criticizing our life. But I saw it as, I don't know, letting off steam, I guess, steam that would make me explode if I didn't get it out.

This is not a pretty picture. Indeed a marriage sustained under the circumstances Michael and Adrian describe would be a life sentence in prison for the partners. It is clear that after 16 years many of the positive features of Adrian and Michael's relationship had been lost in the atmosphere of irritation that these two shared. Because this pattern went on for too long, the couple found that the irritation literally became their relationship and Michael was ready to walk out in exasperation.

We all know that, as Adrian says, when people live together, disagreements are inevitable. What happened in Adrian and Michael's case, then? Was the deterioration of their once-loving relationahip simply the expected result of living together? Is intimacy the inevitable victim of what some might call the "overexposure" of marriage partners to each other? Many people who are opposed to marriage and who decry it as a limiting way of life would answer yes to these questions, but my own answer is an emphatic *no*. The fact is, Adrian and Michael were destroying their marriage out of ignorance— ignorance of the importance of communication and the technique of *effective argumentation*.

SHATTERING THE MYTHS

Let us look closely at the truism that when people live together, disagreements are inevitable. I would like to elaborate on this notion by suggesting that not only are disagreements inevitable, but to a greater or lesser degree, they are continual. That is, when people make an effort to "work things out," they cannot, or should not, expect to put an end to all disagreements once and for all. Such a plan is doomed to failure. A marriage consists of two people who bring to the relationship their own values, desires, priorities, and concerns, not to mention a unique body of experience that influences their approach to life. Two people whose values, priorities, backgrounds, and so on are similar are likely to have fewer disagreements than two who differ radically. Similarity of backgrounds, however, by no means eliminates disagreements from a marriage.

Some couples despair at ever working things out, because they believe in the myth that somewhere in the ideal marriage is a plateau to be reached where a husband and wife finally stand linked in perfect compatibility, never to disagree again. In their mistaken belief in this place over the rainbow, free of conflict and discontent, they experience a sense of failure at never reaching the rainbow's end in their own marriages. That sense in itself can undermine the quality of the relationship.

One function of this chapter is to shatter this myth completely. No such never-never land exists; no couple ever suddenly discovered themselves to be in perfect agreement for the rest of their lives. Only in a universe where life suddenly came to a standstill might one find a couple gazing complacently at each other throughout eternity. For us terrestrial beings, life will keep changing, and as it does, disagreements and conflicts are sure to emerge.

What is important for marriage partners to learn, then, is not how to avoid conflict—a futile exercise given the inevitability of disagreement—but rather how to resolve conflict as it arises. The key word here is *learn*, for, again contrary to popular opinion, the capacity of two people to adjust their beliefs and priorities, to reassess existing circumstances, and to take certain actions to become more comfortable is a sophisticated interpersonal skill, not an inborn trait. It is true that some people are naturally better at conflict resolution than others, but even they learn to refine their skill through practice. A second objective of this chapter, then, is to look closely at this skill of conflict resolution, to discover how it works and how it can be developed. One instructive way of accomplishing this goal will be to look at attempts, or nonattempts, at resolution that do not work—at Michael and Adrian's way, for instance.

ARGUMENTATION AS COMMUNICATION

The technique of conflict resolution is not really the rare bird I have perhaps suggested that is is. What the process really is, and the term I'll use for the process from here on, is *effective argumentation.* The thing we are recommending here to replace the never-never-land myth is the good old-fashioned argument, but the argument done right.

The process that Adrian and Michael's descriptions imply is not effective argumentation. Rather they are engaged in a cat-and-mouse game in which the central issue is never touched and its resolution thus becomes impossible. Far from arguing through a conflict, these two are unable even to acknowledge together that a conflict exists. The mere suggestion makes Michael clam up, aghast at the prospect of undergoing not only immediate pain, but also a future full of repeated discomfort. Adrian tries to goad Michael out of his silence, but her exasperation at his avoidance response inhibits her from directly addressing the source of the conflict.

Real, productive arguing is an aspect of the bedrock of strong, healthy marriages: open communication. It is a refinement of the ability to look each other in the eye and speak honestly about feelings, beliefs, one's very basic identity, confident that each partner cares about what the other has to say. Often people begin marriage with a willingness to communicate, but only a limited ability to do so, and this willingness itself is sometimes enough to serve as a strong foundation to the marital relationship. With a desire to remain together and a faith on both partners' parts that they will remain together, the couple can work to evolve a style of communication that suits them as unique individuals in a unique relationship. What they need to realize is that such an evolution really is taking place and that communication really can improve over time for couples who remain willing to work at it.

The same is true for the special branch of communication we are calling argumentation: couples need time to develop a style of arguing that works for them as individuals. They need to learn each other's eccentricities, fears, excesses, and insecurities regarding conflict and to confront each other on the issue in question without giving unnecessary pain.

One of the special hidden advantages of long-term marriages is that the couple's style for resolving conflict has had plenty of time to evolve. Consider Cindy and Brad's marriage, 27 years after their wedding. Said Cindy:

> When we first got married, both of us were terrified, I think, when conflicts arose. We prided ourselves on getting along so

well—you know, all the time marveling at how our thoughts were always so similar, how we'd always be humming the same song, thinking about seeing the same movie, and so on. When one or the other of us had differences of opinion, I think we played it down, maybe even pretended to agree. And I was raised with the idea that the man always had the last word. My mother tried to agree with my father always, and if she didn't, well, it didn't matter much anyway. He always got his way and paid no attention to anyone else's opinion in the family.

But I guess I had a streak of independence in me, because when my babies started coming, I started having very strong opinions and not backing down. Bob's not like my father—not so authoritarian—but he's no wilting violet either; he's got plenty of strong opinions, too. I think we were both surprised to find out how often we disagreed about such things as discipline, eating habits, school work, all those millions of matters that arise when kids enter the scene. And we were amazed at how much we were fighting—yelling even, or worse, steaming around in silence for days. I'd say it took us a few years to get used to the idea that just because we had arguments, it didn't mean we didn't love each other or that our marriage was falling apart. And somehow I came to recognize conflicts before they erupted, and came to know that we'd have to hash them out. Then it didn't seem like the end of the world. I could recognize the signals: Brad would explode, then get silent, then ignore me, then, finally, open up. I would cry, accuse him of ignoring my point of view, as my father ignored my mother's opinions, and of making me feel stupid and of having stupid views. Finally we'd get to the issue and talk about it some late night after going through days of silence about the other stuff not even connected to the original point. And now, after 27 years of marriage, we've finally learned to skip those preliminary steps. We yell at each other a lot still, but I think our arguments are more to the point. Now instead of worrying that arguing means we don't love each other, I just go ahead and say what I mean. So we disagree, so what? Who doesn't?

The pattern Cindy describes is not at all uncommon. Many newlyweds downplay conflict or try to diminish its presence in their relationship. By means of courtesy and a certain amount of self-deceit, they can indeed manage to convince themselves that "Oh, we're best friends; we never disagree."

It is important to note that the opposite mode is also prevalent—that in which newly marrieds find themselves arguing about everything, perhaps overly concerned that everything gets talked about. Often the impetus to such continual battling at the outset of marriage is the partners' fear of losing their individual identities and of "giving in" to the other on their own turf. Such couples often need to learn the art of compromise and self-control to reduce the frequency of their confrontations; both skills are aspects of effective argumentation dealt with later in the chapter.

With the passage of time and the growing need to develop a style of living together, mates will usually find themselves disagreeing more. The arrival of children is sure to increase the frequency and intensity of disagreement between the partners, since child rearing not only involves the central core of ourselves, where our basic attitudes and values come into play, but also a multitude of practical considerations that couples without children can avoid. And the presence of children often increases financial pressures as well, another realm in which the potential for disagreement is great. Thus couples with children tend to argue more than those without children. And, to complete an overview of general patterns, middle-aged couples who have grown to know each other and have evolved a style of conflict resolution together tend to argue less and to suffer fewer scars than less experienced couples when they do come into conflict.

This pattern depends, of course, on a widening communication between the partners over time. Open communication is a component in the successful long-term marriage for which most people in our society have received shockingly poor training, even in expressing themselves to their loved ones. It is safe to say that poorly developed communication skills are associated with many problems in interpersonal relations, and particularly with those problems most frequently experienced in marriage.

About Accommodation

Arthur and Ann view their 25-year marrige as a happy and successful one with both partners having put continuing energy into building a mutually satisfying life. Arthur in particular sees marriage as a whole as a matter of compromise—or perhaps accommodation is the better word, implying, as it does, *adjustment to another's needs or interests*, rather than giving in. He describes himself as asking himself often, "How important is it to me that I have my own way right now?" and as answering very often, "Not very important at all." He feels that this slight pause when new issues arise between Ann and himself is responsible for the even-tempered character of their household. At the same time, he hastens to add that when he does have strong feelings on a subject he is careful to express them and unwilling to conciliate for the sake of avoiding trouble. But he does insist that when two people live together and want to continue living together, compromise—accommodation—is a necessary ingredient. "It's what makes our marriage work," he told me. "Compromise *plus* respect for each other's right to hold separate opinions. I think we expect to have different opinions sometimes, and compromising then becomes a loving act—a conscious search for a way to get back on track. But we do know that each of us must get enough of what we want included in the compromise for it to feel good in the long run."

Some Stoppers

Do the following sound familiar to you? "I've had this on my mind for a long time but somehow I've never found the right time to bring it up." "I don't want to spoil the good time we're having by bringing up what's troubling me. It's not worth upsetting the applecart." "He might leave me if I nag him too much. I'm afraid to bring it up." And finally, "If I tell my wife she does something I don't like, she says I'm always criticizing her. If I say nothing, she says I never talk to her. If I disagree with her, she says I always take the opposite side but if I say nothing, she keeps asking me what I think and why I don't ever tell her what's on my mind. What's a guy to do?"

All these familiar expressions reflect a reluctance to communicate with the marriage partner. And yet in marriage, as in all close relationships, to be intimate is to communicate, and to communicate is to risk disagreement in the interest of improving mutual understanding. Those who refuse to take the risk, who are afraid to endanger what little they have together for the sake of enriching their bond, find, like Michael and Adrian, that intimacy diminishes and eventually the tie is broken. Those who do take the risk, and invest time and energy in expressing themselves honestly and in discovering their partner's true feelings, begin to change the patterns that do not work for them and to evolve their own style of conflict resolution.

Important work has to be done in finding ground on which both people feel comfortable, recognizing that in rare instances there will indeed be no zone of comfort. In fact, if couples are unable to reach a reasonable middle ground in most of their difficulties, their whole marriage is probably on shaky ground. But those people who believe in the rightness of their marriage and are optimistic about their potential success in living together over the long run are often able, with experience, to change behavior patterns that do not mesh and to do the communication work necessary to create a productive style of arguing.

THE FEAR OF ANGER

As a child Joe learned to associate anger with abandonment. At the height of his parents' arguments, his father would invariably reach a new pitch of fury and stomp out the door, to return perhaps two days, perhaps two months, later. Joe was always fearful that his dad, whom he loved very much, would never return. When he grew up, the very first signs of anger in those close to him triggered anxiety (expressed as pain in his chest) and an urge to conciliate or compromise to end the episode. He married an exceptionally mild-mannered woman, Alice, but was surprised early in the marriage to learn of her unexpected spunk at demanding what she considered "only right." With none of her husband's fear of anger, Alice was always ready to argue vigorously when they disagreed, and she was infuriated whenever Joe exhibited what she called his "dishrag side" in an argument. It took many years of marriage and a series of sessions with a psychotherapist for Joe to realize the source of the fear that Alice's anger in arguments aroused in him. It took time for him to accept the notion that his wife's anger did not mean that she was intending to leave him.

Anger is normal between people who love each other, but for those who fear anger—and such fear is usually rooted in childhood experience—attempting to resolve conflict becomes an awesome trial. Intense anger, normal at times, can be very tricky to express without being destructive. All of us have the right to our feelings but none has the right to damage or destroy others for the sake of expressing them. Still, even though difficult, we can all learn to control our anger if we believe that it is necessary and possible to do so. As soon as both partners realize that scathing verbal attacks and physical violence are out of the question, they have established ground rules together and have cleared the path for reasonable discussion. And reasonable discussion, though heated at times, is the most profitable means of resolving differences.

It is possible! It can be done! People locked into years-long patterns of ineffective conflict resolution often consider continual battling the price they pay for remaining married. But with the willingness to work and the faith that the work is worthwhile, couples can achieve a clear and effective arguing style, as evidenced by the subjects in our study.

Beyond this simple framework, couples will find that they need to experiment together, perhaps with the help of a therapist, to develop the ground rules that work for them. However, these simple rules should function in any argument:

1. *No hitting or verbal abuse.* Physical violence and name calling are always destructive and have no place in effective conflict resolution. The point is to resolve a disagreement, not to cause physical or emotional pain.

2. *Develop some key words that can help to defuse a situation.* See if you can agree on a way of suspending an argument when it gets too heated by saying something that does not trigger greater anger. "Can we stop for a few minutes? I'm feeling very upset and would like to calm myself so that we can talk." Or develop a catchword that can lighten the tension, for example, "Truce," "Let's take ten," or "Time," or whatever feels reasonable between the two of you. Talk about how you can reach each other in the height of fury in a way that both of you feel has a reasonable chance of stopping the argument for the moment.

3. *Establish basic rules for arguing.* It is well known that fighters in the ring are not allowed to punch below the belt. You need to define what is below the belt in your life and come to an agreement with each other. Talk about those areas that you both can see as destructive rather than leading to a solution of a problem. Remember that an argument should not be used to hurt, but to reduce tension and to reach a compromise. It does not matter who started the argu-

ment; look to resolve it. Neither partner should feel that there
has been a winner or a loser. If somebody wins, everybody
loses.

4. *Stick to the issue.* Bringing up things from the past
("That's just what I expected you to say; you took the same
position when I wanted to visit my sister") or attacking the
other's character ("You are such a coward! No wonder we're in
this mess—it's all because you're so timid") are ways of avoiding the issue at hand. Such avoidance will guarantee that the
specific conflict will go unresolved. Instead try to ignore these
extraneous items and stay with the issue at hand.

5. *Empathize.* Try to imagine thoroughly your partner's
point of view—Do not be framing your rebuttal. Listen! And
try to understand how your partner feels.

6. *Look for a solution, not a victory.* Remember you are
seeking resolution, and will probably have to create a means
of agreeing together. To resolve conflict is not to crush the
other under a wall of words or a blanket of noise. Rather it is
generally achieved through compromise, which itself grows
out of the exploration and mutual understanding of both partners' points of view. Reaching a compromise means that both
people get enough of what they need or want incorporated in
the solution; then the argument has been effective and has
served its purpose.

Before leaving the topic of conflict-resolution technique, it
is important to note that there are times when argumentation, however "effective" in intent, is inappropriate. A significant aspect of conflict resolution is the ability to recognize
such instances and to suppress the temptation to jump into
the fray. Consider the situation, for example, in which one
person is clearly wrong and the other responds with anger or
irritation that is indisputably justified. Lee, for instance,
warns Sam in the morning that this is the last day to pay for
the car registration without penalty. She offers to do it, but
he promises to take care of it at lunch—and never gives it
another thought for the rest of the day. When Lee learns that
Sam has forgotten and that they now owe more than $50 in
penalty to the motor vehicles department, she is furious and
lashes out. In these circumstances Sam would be wise to take
the tongue-whipping in good grace without trying to defend
himself or, worse, to point out Lee's imperfections in an at-

tempt to get even. Both of these responses no doubt would result in arguments but they would be far from effective—except to breed conflict rather than to resolve it.

Other circumstances plainly call for one or both mates to hold back rather than to confront each other angrily. Consider the man or woman who comes in from a hard day at work, bristling with fury over something that happened during the day. An insecure or unthinking mate might feel personally offended by the irritable tone the former adopts or at the glowering silence that darkens the mood at the dinner table. But the more thoughtful and aware mate will realize that he or she is not the source of the trouble, and will allow the angry one to calm down or to talk it out. It certainly is not the time to air a gripe of one's own. *The real skill lies in discerning when a confrontation would be productive and when it is appropriate to back off.*

Finally, for many people developing a style of conflict resolution might mean realizing that they require some private time away from their partners to clarify their thoughts and feelings about the issue at hand. Some might need this time alone to work up to a productive confrontation. Some might feel confused and uncertain after becoming involved in a discussion and require a break for time alone. The point is that each of us needs to respect our own and our mate's particular ways of handling the stress and high emotion that conflict creates. The need to pause and reflect on the decision, to back off completely where it seems appropriate, is as integral to effective conflict resolution as active confrontation. In all, the art is a subtle one, and its cultivation can go on over the duration of a long and healthy marriage. Again Chaucer reminds us:

In love whoever is the most patient has the advantage. Patience is surely a sovereign virtue: for according to the scholars it conquers where severity achieves nothing. You cannot scold or grumble at every harsh word. Learn forbearance; or you will have to learn it, I swear, whether you will or no; for surely there is nobody in the world who does not behave badly on occasion. Anger, illness, the influence of the stars, wine, grief, or a change of mood very often make one act or speak amiss. You cannot take revenge for every wrong. Everyone who knows how to govern himself must exercise restraint according to circumstances.

A ROGUE'S GALLERY:
HOW NOT TO HAVE AN ARGUMENT

Let us turn now to a survey of some of the more frequently encountered means of failing to argue effectively. The objective here is to demonstrate the weaknesses of these faulty conflict-resolution techniques.

The Pulverizers

Neither Anita nor Al is afraid of conflict. Rather their confrontations usually escalate into uncontrolled verbal abuse almost before they know it. Both have bad tempers, to which they give free rein, and usually both wind up feeling pulverized by the exchange. Needless to say, the original issue goes unresolved, and sometimes is even forgotten, in the mêlée.

"Damn it, Anita," explodes Al, when she asks him whether he has scheduled his vacation yet at work. "You can't let up for a minute, can you? You can't keep you goddam nose out of anything, can you? I told you I'd take care of it and I will—but without your help, so just back off."

"You bastard," growls Anita, narrowing her eyes. "What a miserable man you really are. I should have known what you were like when you told me you were taking this job 12 years ago. That was when you died, Al. Did you know that? You just stopped growing at that point and gave up."

"Just back off, Anita, will you? What kind of a person do you want the kids to think they have for a mother? Somebody who just won't let up? You're just a mean bitch, that's what you are. Born mean and stayed that way."

"I might be mean but you're just nothing, nothing at all. What's it feel like to be nothing, Al?"

After one of their arguments, the air is so heavily clouded with accusations and countercharges, abusive names, and exaggerated complaints that neither Al nor Anita is able to focus on solving the problem at hand. At best the two retreat, licking their wounds and trying to shake off the hurt they sustained. But the residue from each encounter remains—angry feelings that inhibit communication, blot out sexual feelings, and further disrupt the relationship. And of course the original issue, in this case scheduling vacations, remains unresolved, stacked up with other unresolved conflicts that have accumulated over the years, separating the couple like a wedge.

The Superior Being

Those men and women who can feel good only if they feel superior to their mates will always have trouble resolving differences. Let us look at Sean, who grew up in a male-dominated home with three older brothers. When he married Norma, he expected to be the head of the household, finally able to run his own show and to be on top after spending his life on the lowest rung of the family ladder. He relished the idea of having power and found himself continually putting Norma down in front of friends when they were out. During arguments he would attack her housekeeping ability and the way she was raising the children.

"I think we should start thinking about buying a home," Norma said conversationally.

"Look Norma, I just don't want to buy a house now, and that's final," Sean answered aggressively. "It's just not the right time. You know nothing about finances, and particularly our finances. You just want what our friends have, and you can't wait until I'm ready."

"But I was just thinking," Norma went on, still reflective, "how much easier it would be with the children if we were out of this apartment, and I'm ready to economize as much as necessary. Don't you think we have enough for the down payment? I mean, if prices keep going up and up, soon it may be impossible.

"Who earns the money around here? I don't want to be told by you that now's the time as long as I'm bringing it in. Anyway you and the kids would probably wreck any house we bought two months after we moved in and we'd be no better off. You still don't have them pick up their toys and I can't stand living in this mess. What's the big deal that you have so much to do? You're home all day and Donald looks like a ragamuffin when I come home. Why don't you do more about it? You're just like your flighty mother."

"Come on, Sean. I do the best I can. You think it's easy to be home all day with the children? Why don't you try it for a month and see how easy it is?"

Clearly the original issue of buying the house has been forgotten, and Norma has come under fire for being ignorant in financial matters, being a failure as a housekeeper and child rearer, and being the daughter of a "flighty" mother. With her only recourse to defend herself against these charges, the exchange has been more an encounter with a bully than a true attempt at conflict resolution.

The Freeze

The freeze is a common—and, sadly, very effective—way of avoiding conflict and thus avoiding conflict resolution. Here is an example. Dorothy, a housewife, and Teddy, a professor of mathematics, parents of three children, have been married for 28 years, and during all that time Teddy's will has generally prevailed at home. "We have our main arguments over money and the children. At first I yell, then I freeze," says Teddy. "And when he freezes, I freeze," adds his wife. She continues:

Sometimes, but rarely, I yell too, Then after time passes, we talk to each other more calmly. But often we do not get back to the problems, and they just remain unsolved. One of our biggest problems has to do with Teddy's relationship with our daughter, who Teddy can't seem to accept as she is. I always feel in the middle, and somehow when we try to talk about it, Teddy and I never seem able to get very far before we shut down. He can never share any of his inner feelings with me, though for a long time I tried to tell him about my feelings. But, dammit, I won't tell him any more because he won't share with me. So the thing just drags on and on, with our girl Frannie more at odds with her father every day.

The Clam and the Runaway

Two other styles of avoiding conflict are evinced by the *clam*—the individual who shuts up tight in the face of disagreements, usually steadfastly answering "Nothing" when the partner asks "What's wrong?"—and the *runaway*: "My husband always runs out of the room when we get into a fight. He just can't stay still long enough to talk to me and figure out a solution." "My wife dashes out of the house as soon as my voice goes over a whisper. She's just in the car and off. I don't know where she goes, and it makes me mad as hell."

When people flee they may fear their own anger, or feel so frustrated and unable to reach their mates that they see no alternative way to stop the action. Some people become so enraged that they fear that violence from within will be unleashed at their mate. One way to avoid running away is to say how upset you are and ask that the argument stop for now and that talk be resumed when both of you are calmer. Many a man or woman has found himself or herself being followed around the house, hounded by an irate mate determined to be the "winner."

The Sneak Attacker

"Oh, Tom never tells me I look nice. You're so lucky, Ruth," says Beth to her friend, fully within her husband's hearing. She is always getting in little jabs at him when he least expects them. The trouble is, it has never been the compliments that she has cared about; her real concerns have to do with the quality of Tom's feelings for her. But the idea of confronting Tom directly with her insecurities overwhelms Beth and she resorts to the sneak attacks on barely related matters.

The list can go on and on—including the beggar for mercy (who repeatedly pleads, "Please, please...I swear I'll never ask again); the smolderer (smarting from a three-month-old hurt, he or she lashes out in anger at some minor incident); the meany ("You stupid jerk, you never do anything right"); the withholder ("But something's wrong, I can tell." "No, no, everything's fine"). You're likely to spot yourself in this gallery of faulty arguers.

Remember that unexpressed emotion, and expecially unexpressed anger and resentment, can poison a relationship and erode intimacy. Only by productive arguing rooted in an ongoing flow of open communication can conflict within a marriage be resolved. And the attempt to create a style of arguing suitable to the partners' needs can itself become a part of the solution, evidencing as it does each partners' desire to overcome the disagreement and preserve and enrich the marriage.

EXERCISES

1. Answer the following questions as honestly as you can. Do not compare your answers with those of your mate until both of you have completed the list. Then look at your responses and see where you differ.

Talk about the differences as a way of deepening your knowledge of each other.

1 = most of the time

2 = some of the time

3 = rarely or never

	Most	*Some*	*Rarely*
I feel you don't listen to my point of view in our discussions.	1	2	3
I feel overpowered by your loud voice.	1	2	3
I have trouble discussing problems with you when you cry.	1	2	3
I feel you attack me when we have arguments.	1	2	3
You and I see things very differently.	1	2	3
I feel you don't respect my opinion.	1	2	3
After an argument my feelings are hurt.	1	2	3
After an argument it's fun to kiss and make up.	1	2	3
I have trouble getting rid of my angry feelings.	1	2	3
I try not to go to bed angry at you.	1	2	3
I would like you to help me get over my anger.	1	2	3
You are not fair in the way you fight.	1	2	3
I feel I stick to the issue when we argue.	1	2	3
When you are illogical, I get angry.	1	2	3
I feel you will not back off from conflict.	1	2	3
Your teasing bothers me.	1	2	3
I am afraid you will hurt me in anger.	1	2	3
When we argue I feel that you no longer love me.	1	2	3

If you leave the house in anger, I fear you will not return.	1	2	3
I feel we do not talk long enough to solve our problems.	1	2	3
I feel we talk too long when we discuss problems.	1	2	3
I feel you nag me.	1	2	3
I feel I nag you.	1	2	3
I don't know how to approach you about sensitive subjects.	1	2	3

2. Think of a favorite gripe, something that has been bothering you for a long time. Tell your mate how you feel, asking him or her to listen with particular care. Now see if your mate can understand what you feel regardless of whether he or she agrees with you. Talk together about what each of you could do to accommodate the other's point of view.

3. Choose a problem in your marriage that does not seem to lend itself to resolution. Can you and your mate allow each other the right to disagree? Talk about it to understand the opposing view more fully, not to reach an agreement.

4. If you have trouble sticking to the issue, it may help to practice staying on track about less emotionally charged material. Pick a subject, any subject—for example, disciplining the children, spending money, accommodating in-laws, making vacation plans—and try to stay with it for five minutes. That is long enough to give you some beginning practice.

If you find that these steps do not yield greater skills in communicating, you may still be reacting to your mate with the remnants of old feelings that are not now appropriate. It may represent early childhood trauma evoking feelings of terror that leave you speechless, or an underlying anger about areas of your life, or the like. These kinds of blocks to conflict resolution do require help from therapists who can help you understand and work out unceasing, unproductive arguments.

7

LIFE WITH CHILDREN

T HE "PEOPLE PRESSURES" THAT affect marriages come not only from outside the household, but from inside as well. These internal influences are particularly persistent and deeply felt, for they are exerted by the partners' own children. True, childless marriages are not uncommon, but in the well-seasoned marriages investigated in the California study, all the participating couples had at least one child, and the average number of children among subjects was three. The raising of three children represents substantial expenditures of time and money, and it is no wonder that many of the conflicts, as well as the deep pleasures, of married life have children as their focus.

In this chapter we survey the ways married people report childrearing has affected their marriages. One purpose is to suggest how relationships might be affected not only by the presence of children, but by the changes children themselves undergo as they mature. A second intention is to identify and clarify common problems and, if not to pose foolproof solutions, at least to offer an objective view of situations that from inside a marriage often appear insoluble. The third goal is to help couples with older children to look back and identify the origins of certain areas of stress that may have evolved within the marital relationship.

TO HAVE OR HAVE NOT

Getting married and having children was the natural course of events, even as late as 1964, when the shortest of the marriages in our study (18 through 30 years long) began. But there is no disputing that times have changed. Strong arguments can be, and are being, made now for actively choosing not to have children: a lack of time in a two-career household, an agreed-upon belief that overpopulation threatens the well-being of the human race as a whole, the awareness by some that they are reluctant to allow children to intrude on their own lives and the pursuit of their personal goals and satisfactions.

Clearly, couples who cite the last reason are poor candidates for parenthood. It would be foolish to try to persuade them otherwise. But this attitude of complacency—"we're much too happy on our own to bring children into the picture; they'd only mess things up"—is prevalent among people who grew up in perhaps the most child-centered era of American parenthood, the "me" generation, the very generation, as a matter of fact, *created* by the people represented in the California study. These children, born in the 1950s and 1960s, may well benefit from exposure to their parents' feelings on the subject, since it offers such a contrast to their own position. Far from disparaging child rearing as a nuisance or a morass of unwanted trouble, 85 percent of the California study subjects reported currently feeling positive about having had children, suggesting that they were an enriching factor in their lives rather than a hindrance. In the interviews, subjects asserted that their children were well worth the trouble they experienced in raising them, though all admitted that children caused various kinds of turmoil in their lives and put stresses on their marriages.

Ron, a physician married for 30 years, ruminates on the role his own children played in his marital relationship with his wife Joan.

Sex was a central feature of our marriage, an important mode of communication, and it still is today. The fact that it served the function that was so important to us, that of producing children, spills over into the other aspects of sex. You can't be impersonal about sex when you know it served this vital role of creating the children of the marriage. It's probably true that our marriage might not have survived in the absence of children. I think the children were the glue in many circumstances, and had it not been for them during a couple of crisis periods, we might have gone our separate ways.

To Ron children were an important binding force between himself and his wife, and the focus on the children helped them through difficult times in their own relationship.

Ron's attitude might remind some of a common theme prevalent in his generation but now viewed with disfavor by professionals and lay people alike: "staying together for the sake of the children." In the accepted—and, I hold, enlightened—view of today, far too many couples during the '50s and early '60s kept empty, destructive marriages alive merely to provide a two-parent family life, however troubled, for their children. The reasoning was that any nuclear family no matter what its quality was better than divorce. This view has shifted to a more balanced position, endorsed by the psychological community as well as society at large: people should decide to remain together or part on the basis of the quality of their relationship, but where children are involved, careful consideration of their needs and roles is appropriate and necessary. In this context Ron's assertion that his children served as glue to the marriage during hard times, far from suggesting that the children alone were the binding force, is an acknowledgment of their significance as integral parts of the family unit.

Clearly having children is inappropriate in some cases. Where the question of whether or not to have children arises, clear self-knowledge plus empathy is a great aid in resolving the question. For some couples consultation with a psychotherapist might be the only way to a decision with which both partners feel completely comfortable. Many people are so vulnerable to family and social pressures in this area—"When are you two going to make a grandpa of me anyway?" or "Married ten years? How many kids? Hmmm"—that they are unable to admit, even to themselves, that they truly prefer not to procreate. In such instances individual or couple counseling can be of use in helping troubled couples sort out their true feelings from those spawned by guilt or the expectations of others.

THE STRESSES TO EXPECT

Having acknowledged that the question of whether to have children at all is valid, and having further suggested that most partners in a long-term successful marriage come to view child rearing as positive, we can turn now to the other side of the coin, on which are inscribed the countless stresses and strains that marriages inevitably experience owing solely to the presence of children. Even where interviewees were unreservedly enthusiastic about parenthood, no one ever called child rearing easy. We can probably take it for granted, in fact, that all parents everywhere and at all times have gone through bad patches that made them wonder what they had gotten themselves into and why. This section presents an overview of the kinds of stresses children typically place on the marital relationship and some approaches to recognizing and alleviating such pressures.

Jealousy and Resentment

It is important to remember that, as a child grows, the difficulties his or her parents face—as well as the pleasures and satisfactions they experience—change, often becoming more complex as the child's personality begins to assert itself. The early problems, by contrast, can be unrelated to the child as an individual. A very common disturbance faced by parents of a new baby is one of simple adjustment: into the domain of a couple, where before they had limitless time for themselves and each other, comes a very demanding, very vociferous, not very polite stranger, laying claim to their time and attention, and completely disrupting the atmosphere the two had established together.

As Daniel describes it:

> When Allen was born, Myrna and I were totally absorbed in everything he did. But I began to feel that I wasn't getting enough attention and I didn't like the way that I felt. I was ashamed of being jealous of my son. I had read about such things in a college sociology course when I was much younger, and the words had meant nothing to me at that time. But here I was missing Myrna and our old life together. How could I feel jealous of the beautiful baby we both adored? I guess I felt ignored, replaced, unimportant; it felt awful to me and yet I knew that my wife was very busy with all the responsibilities of the house and the baby. But I needed some time too.

That was the first time their baby was to create a problem for Daniel and Myrna, but it certainly was not the last. Daniel felt increasingly terrible; he believed he had no right to resent the time his wife spent with their son and did not feel able to talk about these upsetting feelings with her. Still the exasperation grew. Many times when Daniel felt like making love and Allen would start to cry, an impatience welled up in Daniel that he could not control. He began to feel as if Allen were the enemy, just waiting to interfere with his sex life. For her part Myrna felt tugged between the baby and her husband. She always seemed to be involved with one or the other of them, with virtually no time for herself. For this couple their baby's infancy created tensions between them even though they were both very happy about the prospect of parenthood and had tried to conceive for three years before Myrna became pregnant.

Other, related problems arose as Allen left the newborn stage. Daniel and Myrna loved concerts and sporting events, and when the baby was two months old they began to go out in the evenings, leaving Allen with a sitter. Not infrequently Allen would come down with a slight illness on the nights that they had tickets for some special event. It was never serious, but Myrna felt uncomfortable about leaving even a mildly sick child with a babysitter. She found she could not relax and have a good time if she knew that Allen might need her. In this she was feeling something common to first-time parents—that only the mother or father can really minister to the baby's needs. By the birth of the second child, this misconception is usually cleared up, through the simple measure of finding a sitter on whom the parents can depend to wipe a runny nose.

For Daniel and Myrna, Allen's birth brought conflicts into a marriage that had up to then been relatively troublefree, and the fact that they suddenly felt a strain between them was a shock in itself. They were unused to confronting difficulties since few serious ones had come up before and they had not yet developed a style for dealing with them. Of course, they had no other sound or sensible option, except to acknowledge the trouble openly and to face it as real.

Daniel had to admit to his feelings of resentment, even jealousy, toward his baby son; Myrna had to express her need for her own demand, free time. Most significantly, both Daniel and Myrna had to feel confident that each one wanted to have a reasonable family life together and that there would be time for each of them in their lives. Today there are greater opportunities for a partnership in the caretaking so that both parents can share the parenting and reduce the pressures felt by each partner. People need a belief in a future to put off the pleasures of the moment. For those to whom the future seems a dim prospect, putting off pleasure is more difficult. With a confidence that they will be together in the future, they are more willing to discuss their true feelings. Without such confidence both will feel anxious about ever having their own needs met again. In a marriage in which both partners are openly committed to staying together and riding out the difficulties, both can come to realize that their own concerns are normal and that the intensity of a first-born's infancy will not last forever. If these issues are not handled along the way, they may crop up many years later as unsettled feelings of deprivation.

It is easy to assert the importance of fully acknowledging and tending to one's personal needs, but actually doing these things can be exceedingly difficult when one's sense of parental responsibility is involved. Social pressures, family pressures, and personal expectations can all combine to make one strive to live up to the "ideal parent" image and sacrifice all personal needs as too selfish or self-centered. Consider Jean's story:

I was only 22 years old, and there I was at home with two little boys who needed my attention all the time. My husband Peter wasn't crazy about little ones altogether, and of course he was at the very beginning of his career as an accountant. He used to go away early in the morning and not return until late at night, and even after the boys were asleep, I had nobody to share my days with. It was so confining being with the boys all day. I rarely had a moment for myself. We couldn't afford any household help, so there just wasn't any relief for me. Before the boys were born, we had time to go out together, and were even able to take vacations. All that ended for us when the kids came.

When they got bigger, the children were the cause of most of our arguments—they were such a complication to us. Maybe I'm one of those women who should never have had children at all. Oh, I love having them around now that they're all living away, but they don't make such demands on me anymore, of course, and I finally have enough time for myself. I guess it's pretty selfish to feel this way, but I love having time to do just what I want when I want to and not have to worry about everybody else. I used to feel so suffocated, just waiting for the day when those children would grow up. I worried that the time would never come when I would be able to go off alone and do things for myself. I always dreamed of things I'd do, and now I'm actually getting the chance to do most of them. I play tennis. I take college courses, and go to the library. My life is infinitely easier now. I have moments of solitude that I longed for when the boys were younger, and now I can be with myself and not feel guilty. It's marvelous!

At 46 Jean is just starting to feel a freedom she has been longing for for 24 years! Let us forget for the moment about the overblown sense of "motherhood" that kept Jean from fulfilling her needs not only throughout her sons' boyhood, but throughout their teenage and college years as well. And let us sidestep the related issues of her relationship with her boys and their sense of independence. Instead let us focus on the effects of Jean's choice—for choice it was, at least to some extent—on her relationship with her husband.

Peter was always busy, and it was easy for him to go along with Jean's full-time motherhood. In fact he expected as much, since the social climate of the times reinforced the image of the doting, selfless mother. Thus he never gave much thought to Jean's inner needs or to possible alternatives that could relieve the strain on their marriage. And there was a lot of strain—24 years of buried, unexpressed resentment! It not only poisoned the household atmosphere, but it became the atmosphere in which they lived, and all were affected, not just Peter and Jean. Heavy silence replaced conversation, and bitter, fruitless arguments took the place of productive confrontations. For Jean in her marriage, repressing her true feelings became a way of life. For Peter marriage was a dulled condition that he endured for the sake of his sons' security, giving it as little thought as possible.

These two not only suffered actively, but they missed out on the potential enjoyment they could have taken in their children's development during their formative years. Never did they share the thrill of watching their boys batting their first base hits, solving a math problem, or training a dog. Never did they sit down together and face a thorny problem as a family—difficulty with a teacher perhaps, or a chronic reading problem. Thus over the years the children became Jean's private responsibility, and burden. Peter provided the wherewithal to keep the household going, but off the premises. His office was his real home; he merely came to the house to eat and sleep.

What options did Jean and Peter really have? Given Peter's lack of sensitivity to Jean's situation from the very beginning (and the social climate), most would agree that the initiative for improving the circumstances would have had to come from Jean. But her view of the matter was resigned from the start: "We couldn't afford any outside help." That was the beginning and end of the matter from her view. A housekeeper would surely have alleviated some of the stress, but was this the only possible solution? Surely not. Making good use of babysitters, play groups, child-care exchanges with friends and relatives, and after-school activites could have done much to free Jean's time and to lift the burden from her shoulders. Jean could have, and certainly for her boys' sake should have, acknowledged her children's emerging independence and reveled in it for her own sake as well as their own. Surely it was unnecessary to keep herself totally available to her 10- and 12-year-old sons in the afternoons while they were off pursuing their individual interests. And surely, even from the beginning, she could have arranged for Peter or a sitter to watch the boys one or two evenings a week in order to pursue her own interests.

Such practical measures never seemed tenable to Jean, for a number of reasons. The primary one was her own mother— overly protective during Jean's childhood, overly protective still, and free with her criticism of Jean's behavior whenever her daughter felt the need to concentrate on her own needs. The image of the doting, long-suffering, ever-available mother loomed large in Jean's consciousness, and conscience, all her life. She was completely unable to defy that implacable presence, silent but stalwart, loving but suffocating, even though it went against her natural grain.

Jean was unable to challenge this image of motherhood on her own, but she might have had more success in asserting herself with her husband's help. After all, forging a personal style of life together is what building a household is all about. Sadly her initial resentment toward Peter cut off this powerful source of support. She simply had to wait it out on her own, over 24 seemingly interminable years, and reap the joys of independence, mixed with feelings of regret, at age 46. But had she expressed her discomfort, her longings, her irritations, and her disappointments at the start, thereby risking criticism from her mother, her husband, and even herself, Peter may have come to see the unfairness in her situation and together they may have reached a practical solution. By failing to risk a few arguments, some raised eyebrows, and some uncertainties within herself, Jean consigned herself to the prison she describes.

On Peter's part, of course, empathy was called for, a talent greatly lacking within him. He needed to make a leap of imagination to understand his wife's situation and to look for ways of relieving some of the stress she was feeling. But without being prodded from the outside, by Jean, really to look at her life and acknowledge the constraints she was under, he continued to hold his stereotypical views of a wife's role and to believe them to be accurate and fair.

So we're back to basics once again: communication based on trust and empathy. At issue here is that a newborn baby can interrupt a couple in the formation of their own relationship and can thus weaken the potential trust and empathy between them, *if* the partners let this happen. Simply being aware of this possibility and focusing on building the marital bond during those early years are strong antidotes against the erosion of trust, openness, and empathy. Remember, over the years the children themselves will benefit from the foundation you have built together. To turn away from attentiveness to that foundation when children begin to come is to risk building a complex structure on a very shaky floor.

Conflicts in Parenting Styles

Raising children brings out some of the most deeply rooted primitive feelings, often revealing traits that never would have surfaced otherwise. For example, how often have you known an apparent agnostic or atheist who, as her child approaches school age, evidences an unsuspected body of religious values and beliefs? Or a rather disorganized, undisciplined fellow who, upon the birth of his children, begins to pull himself together and impose order and discipline on his own life and in his household generally? Such reversals are commonplace, and often they bring with them conflicts and changes in the marital relationship.

Millions of decisions go into child raising, and only the very lucky find themselves in agreement with their mates on most or all issues of importance—matters of discipline, education, language, morality, and the like. Couples with the greatest difficulty in reconciling conflicts in parenting styles are usually those from very different backgrounds whose values and ethics differ markedly from each other. Usually such partners must grow and change significantly even to see validity in their mates' point of view. For the rest of us, raising children occasions endless discussions, and often endless compromises, in the effort to resolve discrepancies.

This dialogue occurred in my office:

AUDREY: You're just a pushover, Jack. Those girls know they can get anything they want from you and they just go for it.

JACK: Maybe, but it makes life easier in the long run, you have to agree. I mean, listen to yourself some time, Audrey. You and the girls are at each other's throats from the minute they come home from school until everyone goes to bed. I can't stand the constant arguing, that's all.

AUDREY: But they'll never learn to work for anything at that rate. Don't you see how they've learned to expect anything they want as their due? They're getting to be real spoiled brats. They have to learn that money doesn't grow on trees, that there's a limit to what they can have.

JACK: I never had anything as a kid, and I'm going to give my kids whatever I can and break my neck to do it. That's my pleasure, to give them what I can. Don't try to take that away from me. And stop ruining our time together as a family by carping at those girls every minute of our lives!

AUDREY: Jack, you're mollycoddling them. Believe me, I know happiness doesn't come from things. They need inner discipline, not bigger bedroom sets. I had the most beautiful bedroom sets in the world and I was bored and miserable. I never learned to think independently. I want these girls to make a way for themselves, to choose a life and go after it. Not like me to whom life just happened.

This dialogue was a continuation of a years-long disagreement. It revealed that Jack was using his daughters to make up for what he missed as a child, as a reparation to himself, and that Audrey in turn was responding to him without realizing the depth of his deprived feeling. As the years passed and their daughters matured—which meant, as always, that the child-rearing issues they faced grew more complex—Audrey and Jack became more entrenched in their conflicting positions. Far from seeking to resolve their differences, each sought to prevail by restating personal beliefs more loudly than the other.

Having the dialogue at all was a step in the right direction, but at some point Jack and Audrey each had to give a little. They needed to realize that their daughters were growing up in a household characterized by conflict and discord, and that neither set of beliefs was having its desired effect. The girls dreaded their parents' arguments and had been showing signs of guilt and insecurity for years, fearing their parents would eventually split up and that they would be the cuase. And their fears, though somewhat exaggerated, were not entirely unfounded, since the constant struggle had eroded the strong bond that had characterized Jack and Audrey's marriage in its early years.

To escape their bind, Jack and Audrey had to reorganize their priorities and give attention to their relationship. After all, they were involved in a marriage, not a political campaign. At such times any agreement that warring partners come to is more constructive than continuing the battle. Focusing on the relationship, with the help of a therapist, is sometimes the only solution to end what appears to be an otherwise futile and unstoppable one-upmanship match. For Jack and Audrey, the therapy was the path back to each other.

Too often the marriage itself is neglected in the fray, and spouses turn away from each other in the effort to prove their way with the children the only right way. Parenting together is a partnership that begins in the marriage bond. As the relationships in the California study show, partners in successful long-term marriages are first and foremost individuals, then wives and husbands, then parents. The series is not only a chronological one, but a reflection of priorities as well. Without nurturing the self and the relationship and keeping both healthy, partners can expect a weakening of the foundation, threatening the whole structure of the family. At all times working toward a resolution of conflict about children (or anything else) is preferable to perpetuating a rift. By mutually seeking to establish trust through open communication, husbands and wives can often resolve myriad differences that gradually become diminished in the light of renewed patience and trust.

Special Alliances and Power Struggles

Sometimes, though, conflicts involving children are symptoms of truly irreconcilable differences between the marriage partners. Where this is true, children become the victims in the situation, as in Kim's case.

> It drives me nuts when my mother tells me to find out what my father wants to do, or eat, or where he wants to go. Why can't she ask him herself? I hate it when they don't talk to each other and I'm in the middle. I feel like I'm on a pulley and I never know which direction the pull will come from. When they get mad at each other, it's so dumb. You know they'll have to talk to each other one of these days, so why not now? And I can't stand it when my dad says to me that I like something he knows my mother doesn't like, as though I'm on his side against her. Even if I do like what he says, I won't admit it because I hate what he's doing.

Kim, at 15, was lucky to be able to vent her frustration at being used. Younger children, unaware of their blamelessness in their parents' ongoing battle, live in misery and confusion as they are pulled this way and that by parents struggling for preeminence. It took her parents two more years before they realized their marriage was not worth saving and that they would do better to go their separate ways. During those two difficult years, Kim felt the tug-of-war ever more acutely, and when she left home in a rage at 17, she carried with her a very negative view of marriage and of male–female relations in general. She was a victim of her parents' inability to deal with problems in their marriage, or even to focus on them directly.

In the course of divorce, parents often fail to realize that their children become the unwilling participants in their struggles against one another. The prelude to the divorce can be as devastating to children as the actual time of the split.

Living Through Children

Another problem is equally common, and in the long run perhaps equally destructive, to both parents and children: that of parents living their lives through their children. In a sense this syndrome is a first cousin to that described above, for again the child is forced to be more than just himself or herself, and must carry the responsibility for living out the fantasies of the parents and bringing home their satisfactions. To encourage, to praise, and to nurture a child as he or she is, is to be a valuable parent who is not living through the child. Then the child can gain a sense of ability and mastery, as well as the freedom to use the skills he or she has, or to focus on building others without risking a breach with the parents. The father who must have an athletic son or the mother who needs her daughter to become a lawyer fails the child if that child is not allowed to seek his or her own natural abilities. Here is Benton's story, told nearly 30 years after the events he describes took place.

My mother hated being a housewife and my father hated his job. Neither of them liked the "ordinariness" of life, if you know what I mean. They wanted something exotic and exciting and never could reconcile themselves to winding up in the suburbs like everyone else they knew. So they sent my sister to acting school and made me take violin lessons—they started us both at age four and never let up until we left the house. I started feeling as if they wouldn't love me unless I played the violin very, very well, and in fact at 40 years old, with a successful law practice thriving, I still feel I've let them down by giving it up. They still make fun of my sister for "throwing away her career" to have babies. I'm angry about that. If they wanted something different in life, why didn't they get it for themselves instead of staying home timidly and making us get it for them?

Another story conveys what is perhaps a more typical manifestation of this overidentification with children. A set of parents came to me with some child-rearing problems that they considered quite serious. Their preadolescent son was talkative in school, was not getting the kind of grades they thought he was capable of getting, and was uncooperative around the house. Both parents were taking the full responsibility for the boy's difficulties and felt that they had to "do something" to help him function better. Their disappointment in the boy was keen, as was their sense of failure as parents. This child improved markedly over time as the parents remained in therapy and gradually gave up the notion that they were totally responsible for who he was and would be. By the time he was a senior in high school, they were able to allow him to do well or poorly, with the understanding that he would take the consequences of his actions. They learned to point out possible behaviors along with possible outcomes while giving the boy freedom to decide what sort of person he wanted to be. His life became his own, not his parents', and the same was true of his successes and failures.

The job of parents is to provide reasonable guidance to their children, not to live life for them, or to see that they make no mistakes. Children should have the privilege of making their own errors in life. It can hurt to watch children make important errors, but that is how all people grow—by testing, making mistakes, taking a new route, succeeding, or failing and trying again.

Not only do children need to be allowed to be individuals, but, as noted before, parents need to remember that they are more than just parents. They are also individuals and marriage partners—as well as sons, daughters, workers, professionals, teammates, and so on. The parents in these two stories saw all their satisfactions in life as stemming from their roles as parents. Not only were they bound to be disappointed, but their functioning as individuals and as mates was bound to be less effective.

An individual's life and marriage do not end when he or she becomes a parent. Those who act as if they do, by neglecting their own needs as adults and their own and their spouses' needs as partners, will experience a lack of fulfillment no matter how dazzling their children's success.

Adolescence

As children grow the issues their parents face become more complex. Perhaps the climax of this gradual increase in complexity comes when the children reach adolescence. At this time children's challenging of parental limits and testing of their own newly emerging identities can result in strains of a whole new order and intensity. The range of difficulties is enormous—from teenagers' mild but galling disrespect of their parents, expressed in a continual tone of sarcasm and reflective of their desire to distance themselves from their parents, to the horrors of drug and sexual abuse, teenage pregnancy, and teenage depression and suicide. Particularly in cases where parents have serious unresolved conflicts left over from their own adolescence, these onslaughts of turmoil can be devastating. Here again, the importance of the parents' solid grounding in their own identities and their own marital relationship cannot be overstated, for without such grounding, they risk being swept into the emotional whirlwind that surrounds their teenagers. Let us look at two stories that embody two contrasting approaches to similar situations.

Laurel and Bill knew that 17-year-old Julie was probably sexually active but they avoided discussing sexuality with her, partly out of shyness, partly because their own sex life had been waning steadily for years and it had been their practice to avoid the issue between themselves as well. After such a long silence on the subject, they found it impossible to break through their personal inhibitions to talk freely with Julie. But when their daughter became pregnant, they could no longer avoid the topic. Something had to be done, some course of action settled upon. Julie was in love and wanted to keep the baby. Laurel favored abortion, and Bill, morally opposed to abortion, argued fiercely for Julie's having the baby and giving it up for adoption. All held tenaciously to their positions, and whenever the three of them sat down to discuss the matter, a full-blown argument, with tears, shouts, and slamming doors, was the inevitable result. The worst part was that Laurel and Bill found themselves more deeply estranged from each other than ever before. Alone together they were utterly unable to broach the subject of Julie's pregnancy—resentment, rage, and feelings of futility inhibited them from even trying. Thus instead of giving strength to each other and thereby offering their daughter the support and guidance she needed and secretly craved, they held out in isolated misery, feeling that the pregnancy put too great a strain on their already weakened family ties. These feelings were borne out, for eventually, in her loneliness, Julie eloped with the child's father, only to be abandoned before the child's birth, and Laurel and Bill separated, both blaming the other for "ruining" their daughter.

In a contrasting situation, Jim and Cathy were taken totally by surprise when their "model" teenage son Mark—intelligent, self-possessed, interested, and active in a variety of things—was discovered by the high school counselor to have a serious drug problem. Far beyond the "experimental" stage, Mark had been buying and selling drugs at school for two years in order to support his own incessant drug use. The parents were shattered and deeply guilt ridden by the notion that they had remained unaware of part of their son's character and the nature of his activities for so long. The accomplishments they were so proud of were misleading; the poise and good humor were a sham. They each felt responsible and foolish, and even more ashamed at their resentment at Mark for playing them for fools.

At first they were too shaken even to consider what they might do, but soon Cathy realized that their sense of helplessness was paralyzing them and that things could only deteriorate as long as they remained inactive. Mark himself seemed sorry enough to have hurt his parents, but there was no indication that he would give up drugs or his trafficking activities simply because his counselor and parents had found him out. One day Cathy asked the counselor to recommend a therapist, not for Mark—not yet—but for herself and Jim, to help them to recover from their sense of having been betrayed and to begin garnering their resources so they could focus their energies on helping Mark. After a few sessions of "crisis therapy," in which the two were encouraged to look to themselves and each other for the necessary strength, they realized that their world had not ended. Their value as individuals and the value of their marriage were in no way diminished by the behavior of their son. Together they had the strength and inner resources to weather this difficulty and to offer Mark the support and guidance he needed, even if for a time he refused to take it. Further, they learned once again, as they often had before in time of trouble, that they were in basic agreement about the way life should be lived, that their partnership was a strong one, and that their love for each other could endure strife, and perhaps even be strengthened by this period of intense family stress. With their own relationship reaffirmed, they were able to work together to gain Mark's trust and eventually to convince him to enter a drug program to end his dependency. Without each other's support, they may never have risked failure in their efforts to help their son.

LIFE IN THE EMPTY NEST

When children leave home in late adolescence, the period of the empty nest follows. This phenomenon has long been touted in both the popular and professional literature, as a sad experience for married couples. The children are gone, they have lives of their own, and mother and dad are desolate. She rattles around aimlessly in the house, and he works perfunctorily through his last days at the office and dreads the moment when he will be retired like an old horse put to pasture.

Well, look again! Things are not quite that bleak in many American households where the children are grown and have left, as stories from various marrieds reveal. As a matter of fact, quite the opposite is true.

Beverly and Charles, married for 30 years, have four children, all grown, some married with children of their own. Here is how Beverly describes the transition when her youngest child left home.

Everyone in the family was worried about it, Stuart, my youngest boy, most of all. He agonized about moving out and couldn't make himself do it. I have to admit I was a little scared about all that freedom looming—I think I was influenced by the soap operas and all those times I myself had thought, "Oh poor woman" when some friend's youngest child left home. But Stu was really hanging around too long for his own good— he was 23 with a good job and a steady girlfriend, and still living with his parents, getting to be an oddball among his friends. Finally Charles and I sat down with him and gently told him it was time to go, that we didn't need protecting, we had each other, and frankly we were looking forward to some time together alone. I don't know if he believed us, or even if we believed ourselves, but he took the hint and rented an apartment.

Meanwhile we began to have a ball. With no more teeth to straighten, college to pay for, and so on, we felt flush. We decided to sell the house and buy a condo ourselves and spent a year doing it over in a very adult way, just to our taste. For the first time, we planned a household together without having to make arrangements for children, and it was a fabulous experience.

I'll tell you, I don't think we knew we had it in us, but we've just been having a ball. Charles is more relaxed around other folks than he's ever been and, well, satisfied, seeing our kids as evidence of a job well done. We raised them well to live on their own; we don't have to worry about them anymore, and we're living to please ourselves now. Sometimes for dinner we have take-out food in front of the TV—something I'd never dreamed of doing when the kids lived with us. We always had a sit-down dinner at the table together. But now—well, who's to see, right?

Doris and Milt have been married for 23 years. Doris' empty-nest story is slightly different.

All during our marriage we were both secretly frustrated workaholics. I didn't know this about myself, but we sure did know it about Milt. He's a photographer with his own studio, and it just used to kill him to stop what he was doing at 5:30 every day and come home. Yet he felt responsible to us, to spend evenings with me and the kids, and guilty if he stayed away too much. And we'd always had the kids—I had Jerry in our first year of marriage and Linda was born in our second. Milt felt pulled away from his work all that time, until the kids moved out to go to college two years ago. For much of our marriage, I worked, but at part-time jobs, receptionist usually, nothing I was enamored with. But in the kids' last years of high school, I decided to finish the training I'd interrupted when I got married and went back to school to become a CPA. When I got my license, I set up my own business with one or two clients— small businesses that needed their books straightened out, and now I'm turning clients down. I do only as much work as I can handle myself at home; I don't want the hassle or intrusion of overseeing employees or working with someone else. And it's great! I love it. Milt's proud of me, and he feels free to put long hours into his business.

Maybe the best part of all is the way we relate to each other now. It reminds me of when we first met and were so full of what we were doing and excited about what we were going to do. A lot of time we meet two or three evenings a week for dinner out so I don't have to cook and it's a little like we're dating or first starting off. We just talk and talk about our work, get excited for each other, each really interested in what the other is doing. It's the most gratifying time of my life!

One more story, that of Marilyn and David, rounds out the picture, because it challenges another myth, that of reluctant retirement. Says David:

I think we both wondered, if not dreaded, what things would be like with the children gone and me at home all the time. All three kids left at once and within the year I was retired—but the first thing was I felt Marilyn relaxing. She's always been one to have her things just so, and with the kids around she always had to struggle with her nerves—good kids, but they messed the house up all the time. Now she felt more comfortable. She'd put the house in order and it would stay that way all day. I appreciated the orderliness of it and kept mostly out of her way as I got more deeply into my painting. I found I couldn't get enough of it and soon started to take classes. I took the cue from Marilyn, who had begun to study antiques.

She reads about them all the time and now she's an expert, could write her own book, I think. It's a real creative time for both of us, and independent in a way, too. Marilyn goes off alone on long trips to visit the kids and grandkids, leaving me home to paint. We never really separated before for any length of time, and she never traveled alone when we were younger. The trips have had an added benefit: we miss each other and feel pretty sexy when we get back together, so somehow or other our sex life has become more interesting than it ever was when the house was full of teenagers.

These stories are not exceptions to the rule; they are reflective of the strong bonds between the partners involved and between them and their children. Certainly no one will deny that it's painful for parents to realize that their family will never be the same again and that their children are on the way to forming their own families and thus new loyalties. But there is life on the other side of the children's growing years, and often, perhaps because it has been relatively undescribed, it is a life full of surprising rewards and unexpected satisfactions.

When children leave home for college, work, or marriage, many do not leave their parents' lives but rather reach a point of separateness when they are independent adults. The parents can—they must—give up feeling that they have to do something for their children to help them meet the demands of the world. They can let go of the responsibility in the belief that they have done as much as they could to prepare their children for life, leaving it up to the kids to find the right way for themselves. The parents by no means withdraw their interest and support, but they need no longer be involved in the children's daily decisions. Of course, it takes a certain belief in one's children's abilities to feel comfortable about letting go, but plenty of parents have this readiness to trust their children. And even if they do not, they soon learn that they no longer have the control over their children's behavior to justify their active participation in their offspring's concerns, and thus must conclude, however reluctantly, that it is no longer their place to tell the children what to do.

At the moment when they realize they are no longer concerned with the daily events in their children's lives, parents become free to indulge their most selfish fantasies with one another. They can decide at the last minute that they would like to eat out without worrying about anybody else's schedule. They can come home from work and decide that they would like to make love now, leaving dinner for later. They can leave town, read a book from start to finish, move away, start a new business or a new vocation. And all without the intricate planning, saving, and endless balancing of priorities that such changes require in a family with growing children.

In short the newly emancipated parents can experience a great sense of freedom that can trigger new responses, new appetites, and a new sense of fun. This is not to say that all parents impatiently await the departure of their children, although some do, but rather that a pleasant surprise may await them. People who generally had good feelings about themselves and their children and have spent hours fearing losing them can enjoy the separatness while savoring their visits with their children.

Obviously not all married people experience this joy when the nest empties. For those parents whose children move out of the house and out of the vicinity it can, of course, be a painful time of readjustment, of reconciling an unexpected way of life, of losing casual warm times together. Parents and children are called upon to develop other ways of maintaining their connection with one another. Phone calls, letters, and visits can gradually be integrated into their lives and, though not ideal, can be acceptable. Such parents may put new energy into relationships with other young family members or friends and find compensation for the separation from their children.

People for whom the children were the only real link holding the relationship together may feel the desolation associated with the familiar stereotype. With the link gone, their marriage may be thrown into a deep crisis from which it may never recover. But for the large number of married people who love each other, who look forward to remaining with each other, and who consider their child rearing with satisfaction as, to use Charles' words, "a job well done," life can open up in new directions after the kids have gone.

EXERCISES

1. You and your mate should answer the following questions as honestly as you can, and without consultation. After

completing the questions, compare your answers. Discuss the differences in the way you feel.

1 = all or most of the time

2 = sometimes

3 = rarely or never

	Most	Some	Rarely
I feel we have as many children as I want.	1	2	3
I wish we had waited longer to conceive.	1	2	3
Our children give me pleasure.	1	2	3
The children are a great drain.	1	2	3

When our children are grown, I hope _____

_____

	Most	Some	Rarely
I feel we need more time with our children	1	2	3
I want to share child rearing.	1	2	3

Our children disappoint me when _____

_____

_____

	Most	Some	Rarely
I feel like a second-class citizen when the children are around.	1	2	3
I feel my mate is too strict with the children.	1	2	3
I feel my mate is too permissive with the children.	1	2	3
I feel our children manipulate my mate.	1	2	3
I feel our children love my mate more than they love me.	1	2	3

    (1) All the children.

    (2) One child _____

                   (name)

I would like to show more affection
   to our children.
   When our children are hostile, I feel _____

_____

_____

I look forward to our children growing
   up and leaving home.   1   2   3
I feel concerned about being alone
when the children are grown.   1   2   3
I think our children are neat.   1   2   3
Children are greatly overrated.   1   2   3
I believe the "empty nest" may be fun.   1   2   3

2. Talk with your mate about what you hope to experience
in raising children. If your children are adults, talk about the
positives and negatives of having had children. How did it impact on the marriage?

3. What more would you like in relating to your children?
Talk about ways to achieve what you want.

8

PARENTAL INFLUENCE
Exorcising the Ghosts

From TIME TO TIME IN THIS
book I have mentioned ways in which ghosts from the parental home creep into and affect a marriage. Because the influence of one's parents is so profound and the process of evolving a style of being apart from parental influence is so challenging, we focus directly on the topic of parental influence
on marriage in this chapter.

Our parents play a continuing role in our lives forever, regardless of our ages or circumstances, and even regardless of
whether they are living or dead. Long after they have died,
strong parents with a heavy influence over their offspring can
assume the form of an internal voice inhabiting a prominent
position inside their children's heads and participating in—
often interfering in—their daily lives and decisions. And living
parents who have failed to relinquish control over their children can exert formidable pressures on their children's marital relationships: at the other end of the spectrum, parents
can be sources of pleasure in their children's marriages, loving grandparents to their children's children, and good com-
panions to the whole family. Between these extremes lies an
infinite number of possible interconnections among parents,
in-laws, and children, their mates, and their children—some
enriching, some perturbing, some downright destructive to
the well-being of the family.

The work to be done by the partners in a well-seasoned marriage is essentially the work of separating from parental influence and evolving together a personal style of being and living as a couple. But separating here by no means refers to breaking the bonds of love and mutual support between parents and married children. Rather it means deepening one's self-knowledge in order to identify parental influences at work within oneself, to distinguish those influences from one's own distinct attitudes and values, and in many instances to resolve conflicts of loyalty that require one to make a choice between pleasing one's parents, one's spouse, and often, one's self.

Each stage of marriage, from the honeymoon to the ripening years of a well-tested relationship, carries with it its own links (varying in strength) to the parental home. In an effort to comprehend the complexity of the interactions between parents, their married children, and their children's mates, let us turn to some case-study sketches demonstrating how parental influences can affect the marital relationship. We begin at the beginning, with the way one's parents can affect the mysterious process of mate selection.

WHO TURNS YOU ON—AND WHY?

That old adage "there's no accounting for taste" is confirmed for all of us time and again. Most of us experience our attractions to certain people as being not too different from our inclinations toward certain things (say, food, cars, clothes, houses), a matter of preference associated with the personal style we have developed over the years. In fact our sense of whom we find appealing, both sexually and socially, is shaped at least in part by the feelings we have had for men and women who were important to us in our early lives, primarily our mothers and fathers—for who has more significance for children? Very often, when a relationship with a parent or other significant adult in childhood was loving and pleasureful, we unconsciously seek to replicate it by choosing a mate with personality traits similar to those of the original individual. Thus though consciously we have little or no awareness of the logic of our choices, we are often drawn to people who touch a chord of memory somewhere deep inside us. These people might arouse us sexually and engage our interest more intensely than anyone else in our adult experience. Unbeknown to us, experiences that we consider to be ancient history and irrelevent to our current lives have actually heavily influenced our choice of mate and thereby the course of our married life.

Conversely, when the significant relationship was a negative one, freighted with pain and frustration, our desires might be aroused only by people whose personality traits are, or are perceived by us to be, in direct contrast to those of the significant adult in our pasts. People who might seem to others to be appealing leave us cold, as within ourselves we recoil from repeating long-forgotten experiences that caused us discomfort as children.

Such influences, whether positive or negative, are not always unconscious. Many people know that their experiences with their parents heavily influenced their choice of mate. Even where such self-knowledge exists, however, it may be distorted. One woman in therapy with me told me she had consciously chosen to marry a man like her father, only to discover as time passed that "I had married my mother." Her husband and mother shared many personality traits and her married life duplicated her childhood family life in many respects. This woman had to do some active exploration of her self and her marriage and feel that she and her husband were responding fully and directly to each other, not to intervening ghosts.

It also happens that men and women consciously choose to marry someone distinctly unlike a particular individual only to discover, well into the marriage, that they have done exactly the opposite. The power of our early experience to influence our feelings is easy to underestimate and hard to defy as in the case of Sonya upon meeting the man she eventually married.

I was a rebellious girl and wanted no part of my father's values, particularly his religion, Judaism, and his profession, which was law. All through high school, I made a big point of going out with non-Jewish athletic boys who had no career plans and hardly the kind of brains that would land them in law school. I dated plenty of them then and continued to go out with men of the same type for a few years after high school. My friends and

family just couldn't believe it when I started going out with a
bookworm like Walt. He'd never held a football in his life; he
was thin and pale, totally unathletic looking; he was a religious
Jew and serious just like my dad; and he was planning to be a
lawyer. I paid no attention to the similarities at the time,
though. I was too busy falling in love. Our first date was like a
miracle—I just flipped by the middle of the evening. I had never
had such a reaction on a date before. I just felt so at ease with
Walt that I had a fabulous time. That was it! We were married
within a year.

In another story, that of Frances, we can discern a young
woman's healthy withdrawal from her father, the best-loved
person in her life until then, as she reached adolescence. As a
child Frances delighted in being with her dad, and took pleasure in outings with him alone, without her sister and
brother. He treated her with a special kind of gentleness that
made her feel important to him. But as she reached her teenage years, Frances began to prefer being with her friends.
Maybe her dad was not quite as perfect as she had believed
after all. She found that certain things he did annoyed her,
and that she was getting into arguments with him as never
before. These arguments and bristling irritations were all part
of a healthy bid for independence, a temporary denial of her
father's value as she began to relate to men of her own generation. The unconscious need to separate from that strong
bond with her dad produced feelings and behavior that defied
logic and mystified both Frances and her dad.

Over the years Frances had an opportunity to date a variety of men, some sharing characteristics of her father, but
rarely bearing any similarity to him in looks or stature.
Gradually Frances stopped denigrating her father and again
felt aware of his strengths and value. She began actively to
hope that her own husband, whoever he might be, would
treat her with the sweetness and respect her father so easily
showed her mother, and she gradually viewed the special
bond between her parents with admiration.

Frances was ready to marry when she met Jason, her husband now of 23 years, and she fell for him quickly and with
great certainty. Many years later she realized that Jason indeed had possessed the qualities that she had always wanted
in a man, qualities that her father had exemplified throughout her childhood. Thus the intense attraction she felt for
Jason when they met was reinforced by a sense of certainty

that this was indeed Mr. Right, the man who matched an image she carried within her.

Freud, of course, has written with genius on the intertwinings in our psyches of the images of our parents and our sexual partners. Many psychological thinkers follow him to this day, writing and commenting about his ideas on this subject. But for our purposes, these few sketches suffice to confirm the powerful unconscious influence our parents can have on our choices of mates simply by the way they exist in our lives and memories.

PARENTAL MODELS

Our childhood experiences within the family not only affect our choice of mate, but also have important influences on our understanding of ourselves as men and women, husbands and wives, and mothers and fathers. It is not unusual for people to adopt the roles that their parents played in their childhood homes and to organize their own households roughly along the lines of those in which they grew up. Too few people enter marriage with conscious ideas about the roles they will play, and most unconsciously rely on their home experiences as guides in one way or another. A great risk in trying to replay such roles is that the two sets of roles brought to the marriage by the two partners will clash. But even where the roles mesh well, the danger remains that the couple will play out their marriage on the known territory of the past, never exploring their own needs and potentials— apart from the learned roles of "husband" and "wife"—to the point of shaping their marriage to suit them both as adults. It is true that the changes in women's roles over the past two decades has spurred a new interest in sex roles and styles within marriage, but evidence of the difficulty people have in evolving personal roles and styles that satisfy their individual needs continues to emerge. Consider Richard and Ann's description of their marriage.

RICHARD: I had no idea about what marriage was going to be like except what I brought from my family, my mother and father. I guess I'd have to say that I probably modeled myself a lot on what my father was in his marriage—and that was basically as a breadwinner who took a back seat to my mother. I took a secondary role in my marriage from the very start because that's what my father did, and it just felt right to me. By "secondary role" I mean I left the decision making to my wife. She took the responsibility for the house and I brought in the money. It started out that way and stayed that way—it was programmed that way, by me, and I guess I'd have to say that I was programmed that way by my father.

ANN: But basically both our parents' marriages were that way. My mother had always been the dominant one in her household, so I just slipped into the dominant role in my household. But I'll tell you I never really loved the role I was assuming; I didn't really want things to be like that. Consciously I never believed that was the way marriage was supposed to be, and I kind of sniffed at my parents for letting it happen to them. I always wanted my dad to take a stronger role and planned to marry a man who would sort of guide me and the children.

RICHARD: Yes but, good or bad, that's not how things were programmed. I may have been sort of low key at home but I saw my role as breadwinner and I think I've done a more than substantial job as far as that goes. I know I've had shortcomings—I'm not as close to the children as I could be, I know that, but after all I wasn't running around, I was out there making money.

This couple stayed on safe ground during their 23-year marriage by living out their family life as their parents had done. They never suffered a major breach, never considered their marriage troubled, but their interviews reveal wistful dissatisfactions. How much more responsive their marriage could have been—how much more dynamic and fulfilling—had they consciously worked together to create their marriage by getting to know themselves and each other and shaping their relationship accordingly.

Richard and Ann's tendency to take on the roles of their parental models had a negative effect on their marriage overall, but, as we saw in Frances' case, one can appreciate the way one's parents functioned as husband and wife and benefit from that appreciation later on. Steve, a man of 36, describes how his parents' marriage looked to him when he was growing up.

My folks had a wonderful relationship. I think they were very happy with each other. My father was the boss...no, he thought he was the boss. My mom had the knack of getting what she wanted but still making him feel that he had too. She wasn't the type to say "do this, do that," but she seemed satisfied with how things were and wasn't afraid to speak up when something was on her mind. They had a mutual understanding that was really very nice, a give-and-take kind of thing. They didn't fight much; they just worked things out between themselves. Since Mom died and I've been married, my father has been an influence on me—I think about what he would do in a given situation when I'm trying to work things out. Both my wife and I ask him to advise occasionally and he offers the occasional opinion, but he'd never say, like some parents do, "Look, this is the smart way to do things."

Steve had warm memories of his parents' relationship and looked forward to being married and sharing his life with a woman who would give him as much pleasure as his own parents had given each other. Thus the image of his parents' marriage was very much alive in him in his dating years when he was actively looking for a mate.

Steve's parents clearly served as "positive models," but for many people parents can be "negative models," the kinds of husbands and wives the subjects distinctly do not want to be. People with this image of their parents often use their family of origin as a sort of reverse mirror in creating a picture of what they want their married lives to be. Many people who swear never to repeat the mistakes of their parents in their relationships with their mates and children find themselves doing so unwittingly and infuriatingly nevertheless. For some the repetitions result from an unconscious need to reenact their parents' failure in a vain attempt to repair it. For others, the repetitions indicate the partners' lack of self-knowledge, lack of inner resources in gaining command of their individual lives, or sense of resignation that, as Richard said repeatedly, "This is the way it was programmed, that's all."

Still many people do follow their inclinations to profit by what they consider their parents' bad example and avoid the pitfalls in marriage they learned to recognize in childhood. Brenda and Leonard, for example, have been married for 25 years. Though they looked forward to being together, both recall approaching marriage with a certain wariness based on their parents' concept of marriage. It was important to Brenda's mother that her daughter "marry well," but the idea of marrying for money was the farthest thing from Brenda's mind. As for Leonard, he had long believed that his parents had little in common with one another other than their children and thought that they had remained married to each other only out of inertia and the fear of loneliness. Brenda and Leonard were outspoken with each other from the beginning of their engagement regarding both their desire to have very different marriages from those of their parents and in their commitment to investing time, energy, and thought into achieving their mutual goal.

> LEONARD: I not only expected, I insisted, that our life be different from both our families' lives. If I thought their way was what marriage was all about, I would never have married at all. But I believed that Brenda and I could make it different—in the way we related to each other and to other people, in our values, in our involvement in events around us, and in our relations with family particularly. With my parents their relations with their own families were terrible—there was animosity, jealousy, envy, bitterness, feuds. I couldn't stand the yelling and so forth when I was growing up and I vowed never to get involved in anything like that on my own.
>
> As for the way my parents related to each other, well, I think they were fond of each other and they treated each other with respect, but to me that's not enough. They had few real friends, few real interests; all in all it seemed a narrow life, not what I had in mind for myself at all. Their marriage wasn't broad or deep enough for me. It just wouldn't have been fulfilling enough. I'm sure when I met Brenda I was consciously looking for a woman with a quick mind, lots of interests, and a real aversion to staying home and devoting her life to her kids.

> BRENDA: My parents believed in being warm and demonstrative, open with their feelings, no holds barred, but to me the atmosphere was always smothering. I retreated from it, couldn't take the attention. I think it made me a very self-contained person because I never liked to tell them what I was doing, what I was interested in, since they already seemed so overly involved as it was. And I started getting a notion early of the kind of man I wanted to marry—he had to be interested in his work, and in my work too. In fact Len and I have one of the most successful two-career households I've ever seen, and I really do think it's because we both had some idea of what marriage ought to be like based on our crummy experiences at home.

Both Brenda and Leonard are lawyers and, though they do not work in the same office, they met on a case and were colleagues for a year before they grew more intimate. For 25 years they have taken a keen interest in each other's careers.

Long before the two-career family became a common phenomenon, they had to give careful thought to running their somewhat unconventional household, particularly when their children, twin girls, were born. The fact that both partners worked throughout the marriage gave them the incentive to create an egalitarian relationship in which they shared responsibility evenly, but each step of the way involved questions that their parents had never faced: whether to have children at all, how much and what kind of child care to use, whether to send their children to private or public schools, and, throughout their marriage, how to ensure that their own relationship was not neglected in the welter of activity that constantly surrounded them. It took work, commitment, vigilant attention, and limitless energy to integrate all levels of their busy lives, but the result was a solid, satisfying long-term marriage whose success both partners describe with pride.

Shaking off old patterns and parental influences is never easy, particularly for those with a limited experience of other ways. But old patterns can be changed, old habits of mind broken. Nothing adds more strength to the marriage bond than a pledge of both partners to put energy into their relationship together, molding it to suit their needs and their tastes. This shaping process is fed by the factors I have identified as prerequisites for the well-seasoned marriage—constantly growing self-knowledge, warm sexuality, deepening empathy, open communication, trust between two equal people, and the active desire to remain married. This commitment of energy toward growth is well suited to the long-term marriage, since it is never an easy or quick operation to shape a marriage to meet the needs and expectations of two individuals. At the risk of repeating myself, it is important to stress that creating the relationship together is the real task of the partners in a long-term marriage, one that is never fully accomplished.

As a side note, it is important to try to counteract the impression that parental models, whether positive or negative, are simply followed like blueprints by the succeeding generation. Fashions in styles of living differ markedly from generation to generation, and these changes are incorporated into people's lives even when they adopt their parents' ways unquestioningly. Thus, for instance, many of the parents of our study subjects subscribed to the belief, dictated by the social climate of the day, that publicly expressing too much warmth and affection toward each other was somehow bad. That generation tended therefore to be much less demonstrative compared with the open expression of affection that is sanctioned today. Further, the women and men in this group of subjects were brought up in a time when sexual feelings were strongly repressed and physical sexual activity was greatly constrained and assuredly "private." Their children have come of age in the "permissive society," when people begin engaging in sexual activity at an earlier age than ever before in the United States. The point here is that one can partake of the social atmosphere of the time—showing affection more freely and becoming sexually active at a relatively young age—while still adopting parental models as we have discussed.

SEPARATION: HOW TO ACCOMPLISH IT

We tend to think of adolescence exclusively as the period when children begin to separate from their parents, and of late adolescence and early adulthood as the time when it is accomplished forever. However, as the preceding section made clear, parental influence actually extends much further into our lives. In fact it is probably safe to say that, whatever effect they have, the images of our parents as we perceived them during our childhood remain with us—all our lives. Still there is a great difference between living with such images and constantly being subject to influences and pressures from them. The work of a married couple is to evolve a style of life together that suits them and to nourish and strengthen the bond between them, while gradually divesting themselves of inappropriate parental pressures that thwart the relationship. A growing awareness of the internalized parental images can require some professional help to bring to consciousness.

What is the work of the parents in all this? Where they feel impelled to interfere in their grown children's lives, self-restraint and letting go are the key words. In our culture at least, the child's choice of a marriage partner is his or hers alone. Painful as a child's "poor choice" might be to parents, the latter's side of the separation process is to allow the child the right to make his or her own life decisions—and mistakes. That said, let us acknowledge that many parents feel no obligation to restrain themselves from pressuring their children into choosing the partners they themselves would select. The pressures usually take the form of whom to marry, but they can also take the form of whom not to marry, the latter linked to the great expectations the parent has for the child, expectations that may never be met. What is the child to do in such a case? How to proceed under an onslaught of parental pressure, especially at a time when he or she is looking to the uncertain future, trying to decide on very little firm evidence what is best? These parental undercurrents arouse conflicts in many people as they consider whether or not to marry, surprising them by arising long after they believed they had separated fully from their parents.

Impossible Parental Standards

Some parents simply believe that no one is good enough for their precious offspring. How difficult it is for the children of such parents. To live up to the grandiose notion of themselves with which they have been raised, they need either to find a "superior being" capable of matching the great expectations or make a conscious compromise by choosing a mate they consider to be inferior; neither option is auspicious for beginning a marriage.

Donna's mother was critical of Allan from the first time she met him. Despite the fact that he was a resident in medicine, came from a stable family, and was of the same religion as Donna, her mother suspected him of not being very bright, and she never changed her mind. Nor did she ever keep her suspicion to herself, before or after the marriage. Donna felt very differently (though in angry times during her 19 years with Allan her mother's opinion would flash through her mind and she would wonder, just briefly, if her mother might be right). From the beginning she felt that Allan was a very smart man, that he loved her unconditionally, and that he was the kind of man with whom she wanted to raise a family. In fact in her eyes Allan was the superior being necessary to prove her mother's objection wrong. His inarguably positive qualities enabled Donna to recognize her mother's unchanging opinion for what it was—a smokescreen for her reluctance to relinquish the girl upon whose childhood dependency she had relied to give her own life meaning.

Marshall, at 24, had a more difficult time in sorting out the pressures he was feeling. He had finished school and was just beginning his career as a civil service worker when he met Elizabeth and began going out with her. Elizabeth, having finished college, was ready to marry after two years of dating, and one night she confronted Marshall with the big question: "Do you really want to marry me or are we wasting our time?"

"Is this an ultimatum?" asked Marshall, knowing that she had a right to an answer.

"I guess you could call it something like that. Look, I really want to get married, Marshall, and soon. I have to know how you feel."

"You know, Elizabeth," said Marshall, "my parents have been asking me the same thing. They just think you're great, couldn't have picked a daughter-in-law they'd like better if they had to do it themselves. But I keep wondering if I'm ready. My mother laughs at me and tells me I don't have to wait for that certainty, but I'm still unsure. She keeps telling me I'm going to mess up a good thing. I can't bear the idea of losing you; can't imagine our not being together, but I have a little patch of hesitation that I can't quite ignore."

Very soon after having this conversation, Marshall and Elizabeth were married and they have remained married for 26 years. Over the years, though, Marshall came to believe that he had given in to the external pressures exerted by his wife and his mother and that he had sacrificed his own true feeling—"the little patch of hesitation" he could not quite ignore—and thus had really married too soon. For him, though he was always a responsible and loving husband, the marriage was often characterized by long periods of dissatisfaction and intense longing for more sexual experience.

During the 26th year of the marriage, this feeling grew unbearable and Marshall became involved with a young woman. This was his one and only extramarital affair, but one that convinced him that he indeed had been deprived of the chance to broaden his experience. In reassessing his decision to marry, he realized he had responded to Elizabeth's need for a clear answer and ignored his own doubts. He also concluded that his parents, in their intense desire that he marry Elizabeth, lacked an awareness of his hesitations and were too anxious to have him settled. After thinking things through deeply, Marshall decided to take some time for himself alone and, despite feelings nearly identical to those of 26 years ago on both Elizabeth's and his mother's part, he decided on a temporary separation from his wife. Had he been able to distinguish his own needs from the desires of his fiancée and parents 26 years ago, he believes now that he would never have married when he did.

Meddling

Harry and Sandra thought they needed distance between themselves and their parents.

SANDRA: My parents' opinions mean so much to me that I'm glad we live on opposite coasts. I can see how, if we lived nearby, some really awful problems could arise, since Harry is as strong-minded as they are and I could spend my life, I think, stranded in between, being tugged this way and that. As it is now, my parents and I love each other long distance and Harry and I live as we please.

HARRY: Yes, Sandra's parents are a couple of real do-gooders who tend to have a lot of opinions about everything under the sun, some of which I don't think much of at all. All they want to do is see that everything is all right—not just for themselves, but for their daughter, for me, for the folks down the block, the president, the hungry in Africa, everyone. And in the process of seeing that everything is all right for us, they come in with opinions on how things ought to be done. It's always surprised me how aggressive they are. I'm not used to it; there's never been any interference from my family.

Sandra and Harry, whether they intended to or not, arrived at a happy solution—geographical separation—to a potentially very sticky problem. Sandra herself hints at the conflicts of loyalty she would experience, were her parents to have the chance to interfere in her life more directly. In a sense she admits to having failed to separate emotionally from her parental family, except by agreeing to put many miles between herself and them. In her doing so, we ought to suspect that the necessary soul searching and eventual confronting necessary for her to claim her independence and declare loyalty to her husband still lie in the future for Sandra. Also inevitable for Sandra, should the geographical situation change, are even more acute conflicts with Harry regarding whose opinions would hold more sway for her.

Consider a concrete example of a typical three-way conflict. John and Andrea were ready to send their only child, Charlie, off to school for the first time, and both had pretty much agreed that Charlie would be going to public school. Andrea's parents were horrified; they considered private school the only possible option for their grandchild and feared for his well-being, as well as his educational future, at the metropolitan public school in John and Andrea's neighborhood. During the summer before school was to begin, they gradually lost their initial restraint in bringing the issue up. Their anxiety grew and they finally offered to pay, and then insisted on paying Charlie's tuition at a prestigious grammar school. True, money was at issue—John and Andrea's primary reason for deciding on public school had indeed been financial. But their talks together on the issue also confirmed that they shared a strong commitment to the public school system, a dislike of the idea of private school, and a faith in Charlie's natural ability to adjust well and learn well in any circumstances. However, her parents' insistence shook Andrea's confidence in their decision; even worse, it made John absolutely livid. The upshot was some very serious, very angry and nonproductive yelling matches, centering not on the issue itself, but on personalities: Andrea's "wishy-washiness," her parents' "pushiness," John's "bull-headedness" and inability to accept help gracefully.

It was Andrea finally who came up for air and realized her responsibility in the matter. She saw that she had been swayed from a position in which she still believed. Further, she realized that she and John—not her parents—were Charlie's parents, and that their decision was rightfully the last word on the subject. She told John of her conclusion, and he took it as a renewal of her commitment to him, which it very explicitly was. Together they faced the question of informing Andrea's parents that their decision was final. The strength that Andrea took from the boost her marriage had received when she pulled away from her parents made this meeting easier than she expected. The younger couple was able to be firm but nonargumentative and to express gratitude for the parent's concern while conveying the refusal to brook any more interference in their domestic affairs. The parents came out of the episode with a new respect for their daughter and her husband, and John and Andrea themselves felt closer to each other than ever.

At issue in the preceding example is the lesson that many people learn slowly in marriage: it is possible to transfer one's loyalty to one's mate while still retaining a healthy and affectionate relationship with one's parents. Arthur, a CPA married to Harriet for 22 years, learned this lesson early in his marriage.

> I was an only child. When I married I became aware that unless I was very careful my mother would, consciously or not, try to run our lives. When we were expecting our first child, it became really obvious, and I felt I had to do something to make her back off. She was just bulldozing over our plans for the new baby and telling us how everything had to be done, buying everything she thought we needed, calling every day to check up on what Harriet was eating. One night I went over to my parents' house with Harriet and kind of called a meeting. I told my mom pretty strongly—and I'd never really taken a strong line with her before—that I loved her very much and always would, but that she had to understand that Harriet was number-one woman and that she and I were making decisions about the baby. I told her I felt she was interfering too much and that she would have to stop, and if she didn't, I'd have to make a hard decision. That was it. That was all I said. And it worked. I don't say she didn't give advice as a grandmother, but her tone was different; she didn't have the drive she had before our talk.

Arthur had great clarity regarding the roles his wife and mother played in his life and his own relationship to each of them. His certainty that his wife was his first priority but that he indeed wished to maintain a loving relationship with his mother enabled him to articulate his feelings and to decide exactly what the situation called for—a request that his mother understand his priorities and never attempt to test them. It is to his credit that he managed to say that, and only that, keeping the meeting clear of unnecessary rationalization and overemotional breast-beating. It was a clear solution to a difficult problem and, according to Arthur and Harriet, it laid the foundation for a close relationship with Arthur's parents that rarely waned in 22 years of marriage.

BUILDING RELATIONS WITH IN-LAWS

If the well-seasoned marriage has started to sound like a network of diplomatic relations, hold on: even more delicate negotiations are yet to come. As we have noted in more than one chapter, far from existing in a vacuum, marriage exists in a dynamic social context, and at times the various connections and interconnections with people outside the household exert tugs on one or both partners that strain the marriage relationship. In this section we consider the fact that two, three, or more sets of parents can be involved in a couple's marriage (with divorce and remarriages to contend with) and that the resulting web of family relations often requires a special effort on each partner's part in establishing strong relations with his or her in-laws. Very often one makes such an effort not merely as a gesture of friendliness to the in-laws, but also as an act of love for one's spouse, an acceptance of the people so intimately connected to the chosen husband or wife. Consider what Carolyn, married to Herb for 19 years, has to say on this subject.

> That first year was the hardest. I really had a difficult time winning over my in-laws, getting them to accept me. I didn't blame them—Herb was their only son and they didn't know me very well at all, but things were difficult because their distrust and discomfort really made Herb uncomfortable. He wanted everyone to get along well, and when he saw how they were feeling, he'd get depressed or mad, worried that we'd always be formal and stiff when we got together. It was pretty awful for a while. His mother especially was terribly polite to me, terribly correct, but she never spoke directly to me, always sort of implying that I couldn't have much of interest to say. At times when we'd go walking togehter she and my father-in-law would just sort of squeeze me out; I really had to get kind of forceful and push my way back in.
>
> Herb just hated all this stuff. He wanted to call his parents and give them hell for not loving me automatically and receiving me into the bosom of the family. But I made up my mind to win them over. It's part of my personality to try to get people to like me, and I guess that was part of the challenge. I really worked on it—calling them, inviting them over, asking my mother-in-law out to lunch. I'm not sure I would have succeeded completely in getting them to love me on my own, though. It was the birth of our daughter that did it—they were just overwhelmed by her and they seemed to think I did an all-right job in taking care of her. Still the work I did to get them to like me I did for Herb, and I think he really appreciated it.

Carolyn may have had an unusually patient and forgiving nature, but she also was strong and persistent in her pursuit of a relationship with her in-laws. The fact that she followed through was clear evidence to her husband that to Carolyn the marriage was worth any trouble she took. He recognized that loyalty and appreciated it deeply, particularly since Carolyn brought about a lessening of the strain with his parents—something he never could have accomplished on his own.

In-laws, and especially mothers-in-law, have long received bad press in our society, but like all stereotypes, the caricatures and myths associated with in-laws obscure the wonderful diversity of reality. Many interviewees in the California study reported having rewarding relationships with their parents-in-law, and some felt privileged to experience true "parenting" from their in-laws in a way they never had with their own parents. An example is Edward, a 47-year-old teacher.

> My in-laws were the greatest people in the world. I really felt lucky to know them. It was a very unusual situation, very happy and satisfying, and very different from what I had with my parents. With my in-laws I could talk. My mother-in-law and I would often spend hours working around the house, and my father-in-law too, and we would just talk about anything and everything—problems with business, politics, television, anything. I remember one night when I was griping about something my wife wanted me to do and I just didn't see the point at all. Well, Pop comes over to me all smiles and says, "You know, Ed, I've been married 40 years, so just shut up already and do it why don't you?" We both laughed. I learned a lot from that old guy. I never had anything like that with my own parents; I couldn't really talk to them at all. But with my in-laws it was special, and when I married I really gained a complete family. I've always been grateful for that.

Not everyone finds such fulfillment, of course. In fact it is probably inevitable that some problems will arise, given the complexities of families and the insecurities and uncertainties so often associated with parent–child relations. The important point is that it is possible to establish and maintain stable, loving relations with one's in-laws. Some husbands and wives, out of their own insecurities, have the inappropriate need to be the only significant person in their mate's life and thus put real effort into ending or interrupting their spouse's relations with his or her parents. Such people need to realize that there is no contest, that their mates can love them in a special way while still loving their parents. One woman I talked with gave me a hint about how to be open to feeling good about in-laws. She said that whenever she had unkind thoughts about her mother-in-law, she reminded herself that the other woman after all had brought up the man she loved, and by that deed alone had earned her friendship.

CARING FOR PARENTS IN NEED

In a very real way, the partners in a long-term marriage grow up together. This is one of the joys of the commitment that lasts over time, and perhaps the source of its most profound rewards. As the partners pass through the various stages of their lives together, the social context around them changes as well. Eventually, inevitably, when no premature loss occurs, their own parents grow old. Very often the parents grow needy as well to some degree—needy of financial help, medical care, assistance in conducting their daily lives, or simply emotional support and attentiveness from their children to show that they are loved, appreciated, and enjoyed. When this happens the mates in the well-seasoned marriage find themselves again—was it ever different?—faced with the need to clarify their own stance by communicating freely, empathizing, and finding strength in their marital bond.

How much help should we give to parents in need? What form should it take? How much should we sacrifice as a family in our efforts to help? How can we resolve our own differences about how much to help? Often a parent's neediness can arise quickly, and with it these questions arise, too, to cloud the family atmosphere and trouble the marriage partners. But the tension created by an older parent's needs—or those of a set of parents, or even two sets of parents—does not end there. It seems often to reverberate throughout the whole family, setting everyone off balance and forcing them to ask themselves and each other what they should or must do.

For many older parents, it is dreadful to find that the planning they did for their old age has been insufficient, or their ability to deal with the aging process is limited, and they need to ask for help. In fact for some independent people asking for help becomes the tragedy of old age—and asking for help from their children, toward whom they still feel protective and to whom they still long to offer help, is a terrible insult to their pride. Thus added to the practical difficulties of daily living is the emotional anguish of being forced into a dependent relationship.

The responses from grown children to their parents' needs vary greatly, and it is not unusual to find that one child takes on the major responsibility for the parents' needs. Clearly the child who plays this central role might expect the unshared burden to cause friction in his or her own family. A wife might demand that her husband pressure his siblings into contributing to their parents' care after watching her husband overwork himself to carry the financial burden alone. Or a husband might object to the amount of time his wife devotes to seeing that her parents receive proper medical care, complaining that she no longer attends to the needs of her own family and that she neglects her relationship with her children and himself. And so it goes—the new situation exerts pressures on all members of a family and creates a myriad of problems and subissues in its wake. By talking over the problems, together weighing alternatives, staying aware of each other's feelings, a couple can maintain open communication in a trusting atmosphere. They can then decide what they are reasonably able to do, what they can offer the parents in need, and the marriage is then likely to weather the strain.

One couple from the California study, Beryl and Lou, married for 27 years, described themselves as the "good" children in both of their families, the siblings who always helped out and were always there when needed. Not only did both continue to play this role throughout the years of their marriage, but they both retained deep loving feelings for their parents while their siblings drifted away and appeared to have cooled in their concern. Beryl and Lou genuinely enjoyed visiting their folks and including them in their lives. When their parents began to require late-night emergency-room visits, they naturally helped out.

As the years went on, however, and Beryl's parents in particular needed more care, they both began to feel resentful about her sisters' noticeable reluctance to share the load. Lou started putting pressure on Beryl to bring the matter up with her sisters, but this Beryl adamantly refused to do. She argued that she, with Lou's help, had the strength and the sincere desire to help her parents and that her sisters had had difficult relationships with them. She eventually agreed to try to involve her sisters as much as possible, but she and her husband understood that they themselves would carry the largest share of responsibility for her parents' care. It took lots of talk and hashing it out to arrive at a workable position.

Lou knew his wife and her family well, and though he grumbled about the strain on Beryl and himself, he eventually concluded that Beryl and he were on the right track in enlisting the sisters in taking on some of the load. In some of their discussions, Lou had accused his wife of a childish need to show what a "good girl" she was, but the more he thought about the history of her sisters' relations with their parents, the more he understood the pressure that Beryl felt. In this case, then, shouldering the major burden was the appropriate action because of the realities of the situation. It took long hours of productive discussion between Beryl and Lou for them to feel confident that their decision was right, and that Beryl would make greater efforts to get more participation from her sisters in doing what needed to be done for her parents.

One might guess that a wife of, say, two years would have difficulty indeed in reassuring herself that she was being fair to her husband, her sisters, and her parents. In the course of her 27-year-long marriage, Beryl had accumulated plenty of evidence of Lou's genuine affection and concern for her parents, and she trusted his motives as they batted ideas back and forth. Beryl knew that Lou meant what he said, that he never agreed to a plan only to renege later on. Thus she knew that once they had reached a decision, they could proceed together in a kind of united front, confident that they both respected their agreed-upon stand and would honor their commitments.

The participants in a successful long-term marriage have been through a lot together after 25 or 30 years. The fact that they have passed through the natural stages of life as a couple can be a source of immense satisfaction to them. One woman interviewed in the California study captured this feeling well, expressing the sense of accomplishment she experienced in looking back over her married life:

I was devastated when my mother died. I was 45 years old, my father had been dead for many years, and my mother and I had always been close—in fact she'd lived with Ben, me, and the kids for the last 12 years. I thought I'd never get over losing her, and my life just fell apart for a while after she was gone. I'd taken care of her during her long last illness and felt when she died that I had nothing left to do, what with the children grown and married and Ben so involved with his new company. Slowly, though, I started coming around; it was when my first grandchild was born. The baby just pulled me back into life, I think, and I started seeing how everything fit together. The birth of the baby kind of balanced my mother's death for me and I could see myself and Ben as having moved into the niche that my mother left empty. Suddenly it occurred to me that we were the old ones now—the grandparents, the oldest generation of the family! I think because our relations with our kids and their spouses are so good—we enjoy each other so much—I get a lot of pleasure out of that idea, and I know Ben plays the patriarch bit for all it's worth. I don't know, am I being too poetical? But there's something satisfying about having done it, about raising good kids and progressing onward the way it's supposed to be, the way it's always been. I still miss my mother but I feel her presence in the family, in her rightful place, and the family itself, with all of us in good health and comfortable, knock wood, seems like a thing that we all created together, and the kids and their kids will keep creating, and I feel so proud of Ben and me and what we've done together.

EXERCISES

1. You and your mate should answer these questions separately. After completing the questions, compare your answers and see where the differences lie. Explore the ideas expressed without trying to win your mate over to your point of view. Try to understand what he/she is feeling.

1 = all or most of the time

2 = sometimes

3 = rarely or never

	Most	Some	Rarely
I feel my parents had a satisfying marriage.	1	2	3

I feel my mate's parents had a satisfying marriage.	1	2	3
I would like to have a marriage like the one my parents had.	1	2	3
I would like to have a different kind of marriage than my parents had.	1	2	3
I feel my parents interfered with my marriage.	1	2	3
I feel my mate's parents interfered with my marriage.	1	2	3

I wanted to marry someone like my
mother/father.   Yes   No
If yes, which one   Mother Father

I think my mate is nothing like either of my parents.	1	2	3
I would like to turn to my parents for guidance.	1	2	3
My parents love/loved one another.	1	2	3

My parents have changed in their
relationship.   Yes   No
For the better   Yes   No
For the worse   Yes   No

My mate knows that she/he comes before my parents in my life	1	2	3
My parents understand that my first obligation is to my wife and family	1	2	3
My parents want unreasonable things from me.	1	2	3

What kind?_____

_____

My parents are entitled to some help
from me when they get older.   Yes   No
In what ways? _____

_____

I enjoy visits with my parents.	1	2	3
I do not see enough of my parents.	1	2	3

	Yes	No
I expect my siblings to help support our parents in their old age.	Yes	No

If yes, what kind? _____

I feel my mate does not cooperate in the care of our parents.	1	2	3
I feel my parents accept my mate.	1	2	3
I feel my in-laws do not accept me.	1	2	3
My parents preferred that I marry someone else.	1	2	3
My parents approve of my marriage.	1	2	3
My parents play a positive role with our children.	1	2	3
I feel that I disappointed my parents when I married.	1	2	3

Parenting and parenthood can be fun. It can also be work. Seek to *maximize* the pleasure!

EPILOGUE

MARRIAGE HAS COME IN FOR some bad press over the years, expecially in the past two decades. During this time people have realized that the traditional ways of living are not the only ways, and in this era of experimentation we have seen many alternatives proposed to the conventional marriage and nuclear family—some to cause a momentary flurry of interest in the popular press and then to fade from sight; others to remain as viable options to be explored by thoughtful people sincerely seeking personal fulfillment. Thus many couples now live together without being married. Others develop contractual arrangements to define their relationships. Others seek out or consciously create communal living situations that replicate multigenerational extended families. Still others choose to be alone, remaining celibate or exploring multiple relationships in ways that would be impossible in the conventional monogamous marriage. Those who do marry might sometimes agree to lift the constraints of monogamy and to pursue outside sexual relationships while maintaining the marriage bond. And others agree to celibacy within marriage and various other arrangements to conform to personal needs. This range of alternatives only covers heterosexual relationships; we are seeing more and more marriages and marriage-like arrangements among gay couples.

It has never been the purpose of this book to evaluate these alternatives to marriage or to try to show that the long-term, committed marriage is somehow better or more durable than the newer options. What I have meant to show is that, contrary to often glib assertions in the popular media, there is life in the old ways yet.

That is a well-kept secret, as I intimated at the start of this book. People do not usually broadcast their luck in achieving satisfaction or that elusive quality, happiness in marriage, perhaps because they do not need to. Nevertheless one of the most optimistic findings of our study of people married 18–30 years was that the majority of the subjects reported that they were much happier now in their marriages than they had ever been. Far from feeling bored, couples were still feeling excitement in a dynamic relationship that exceeded their expectations. That is, even these partners in fundamentally healthy and thriving marriages had anticipated a flattening out of their feelings and were gladdened and stimulated to discover, as the years went on, that the opposite was true: their feelings deepened and their marital bond grew stronger over time. They reported a sense that things had never ceased happening to stimulate their feelings about each other and that, overall, the quality of their relationship was highly satisfying.

I hope I have succeeded in bringing attention to the special rewards of a long-term marriage and of demonstrating the gratification that partners can experience in growing up together and partaking in the natural cycles of the generations. The increasing divorce rate, which gets wide attention, points up the fact that family life can be chaotic, overdemanding, and ultimately tenuous, a mass of disappointments and broken promises. But family life, with children or without, has another side to it, too—a quiet side that allows family members to experience a sense of continuity. This palpable link with past and future generations can itself engender a sense that the work involved in building family ties had, in retrospect, been well worth the trouble. This book represents my sincere effort at celebrating this often unsung but deeply rewarding aspect of life.

Marriage—the author's definition: Marriage presents people with the unique opportunity to grow within the context of a nurturing relationship where there is room for autonomy, intimacy, mutual respect, communication, companionship, sharing, and a climate for continual emergence into new stages of living with a loved one with whom one is connected in a special way.

REFERENCES

INTRODUCTION

1. The study referred to as "The California Study" was published in January 1983 in *Social Work*. Reprints are available on request to Gardner Press.

CHAPTER 1

1. References related to the role of *empathy* in marriage: Blanck and Blanck; Blood and Wolfe; Burgess and Locke; Cottrell; Fliegel et al.; Foote and Cottrell; Goodman and Oshe; Greenson; Hicks and Platt; Kirkpatrick and Hobart; Klein; Kohut *(The Analysis of the Self)*; Vernon and Stewart.

2. References on *Consequence of Mate Perception:* Hicks and Platt, Luckey, Sporakowski and Hughston, Waring et al., Wiggins et al.

3. The role of the Oedipal complex: Blanck and Blanc, Eisenstein, Freud (vols. 7, 18, 21, 22), Heiman, Klein.

   References to Chaucer, "The Franklin Tale" in the *Canterbury Tales.*

4. The task of discovering the self appears in the literature throughout: Jacobson, Kohut, Klein, Freud, Erikson, etc.

5. The book is a children's book, *A Hole is to Dig* by Ruth Krauss.

CHAPTER 2

1. The importance of developing and maintaining a sense of self in relationships with others is written about by Blanck and Blanck, Erickson, Freud, Jacobson, Kernberg, Klein, Kohut and Mahler.

   Article: Wexler and Steidl—1978.

2. Excerpt from poem by Robert Burns, "To a Louse."

3. Equality in marriage references: Blood and Wolfe, Burgess et al., Dowling, Lederer and Jackson, O'Neill and O'Neill.

CHAPTER 3

1. General reading: Chessler, Lederer and Jackson, O'Neill and O'Neill, Pahl.

CHAPTER 4

1. References on *Intimacy and Sex*: Ackerman, Erikson, Kaplan, Klein, Levinger, Waring et al.

2. Sexual dysfunction and good functiong: Kaplan, Katchadourian Kinsey, Masters and Johnson, Stoller.

3. Sex and aging: Frank et al., Cuber and Haroff, Terman.

CHAPTER 5

1. The temptations and problems of monogamy are approached by three writers: Freud (vols. 9, 18, and 21 on the "burden" of monogamy), Klein (explaining the meaning of infidelity), O'Neill and O'Neill (seeing possibilities of outside sexual experience done openly).

2. Article: Frankel

3. Trust as it relates to sex: Erikson, Kaplan, O'Neill and O'Neill.

CHAPTER 6

1. References to communication as a factor in the quality of marriage: Ackerman, Cooke, Goodman and Oshe, Hicks and Platt, Karlsson, Rausch et al.

2. Marriages getting better with time: Stinnett.

CHAPTER 7

1. Children as creators of conflict is addressed by Blood and Wolfe.

2. The myth of the negatives of the empty nest is refuted: Lowenthal et al., Rollins and Feldman, Greenberg.

CHAPTER 8

1. The role of the unconscious in mate selection: Blanck and Blanck, Burgess and Wallin, Freud (vols. 7, 22), Hollis, Jung Klien, Komarovsky, McKain, Satir, Strauss, Winch and Goodman.

Bibliography

Ackerman, Nathan W. *The Psychodynamics of Family Life.*
New York: Basic Books, 1958.

Ard, Ben N., Jr. and Ard, Constance Callahan (eds.). *Handbook of Marriage Counseling.* Palo Alto, California: Science and Behavioral Books, 1976.

Argyle, Michael, and Furnham, Adrian. "Sources of Satisfaction and Conflict in Long-term Relationships." *Journal of Marriage and The Family,* Aug. 1983, 45(3), 481–493.

Bahr, Stephen J., Chappell, Bradford C., and Leigh, Geoffrey K. "Age at Marriage, Role Enactment, Role Consensus and Marital Satisfaction." *Journal of Marriage and the Family,* Nov. 1983, 45(4), 795–803.

Bernard, Jessie. *The Future of Marriage.* New York: Bantam Books, 1973.

Betcher, R. W. "Intimate Play and Marital Adaptation." *Psychiatry,* Feb. 1981, 44(1), 13–33.

Blanck, Rubin, and Blanck, Gertrude. *Marriage and Personal Development.* New York: Columbia University Press, 1968.

Blood, Robert O., Jr., and Wolfe, Donald M. *Husbands and Wives,* Glencoe, Ill.: Free Press, 1960.

Bowlby, John. *Attachment and Loss,* Vol. I. New York: Basic Books, 1969.

Burgess, Ernest W., and Locke, Harvey J. *The Family* (2nd ed.). New York: American Book Co, 1960.

Burgess, Ernest W., and Wallin, Paul, with Schultz, Gladys. *Courtship, Engagement and Marriage.* Philadelphia, New York: J. B. Lippincott, 1953, 1954.

Burns, Robert, "To a Louse." Richard Addington (ed.), *The Viking Book of Poetry of the English Speaking World,* Vol. I. New York: Viking Press. 1958.

Chaucer, Geoffrey. The *Canterbury Tales, A Prose Version in Modern English* by David Wright. New York: Vintage Books, 1964.

Christensen, H. T. *Marriage Analysis: Foundations for Successful Family Life* (2nd ed.) New York: Ronald Press, 1958.

Christensen, Harold T. (ed.) *Handbook of Marriage and the Family.* Chicago: Rand McNally, 1964.

Cooke, Phillip W. "A Study of Husband–Wife Behavior and Behavior Changes When Joint Interviewing Is Employed as a Method of Therapy in Marriage Counseling." Univ. of Pennsylvania D.S.W. 1964. Ann Arbor, Mich. University Microfilms Inc.

Cottrell, Leonard. "An Analysis of Situational Fields in Social Psychology," *American Sociological Review,* June 1942, 1(3), 370–383.

Cuber, John F., and Harroff, Peggy. *Sex and the Significant Americans.* Baltimore, Md.: Penguin Books, 1966.

Dowling, Colette. *The Cinderalla Complex.* New York: Summit
Books,1981.

Eisenstein, Victor W. *Neurotic Interaction in Marriage.* New York:
Basic Books, 1956.

Erikson, Erik H. *Childhood and Society* (2nd ed.), New York:
W. W. Norton, 1963.

Field, Dorothy, and Weishaus, Sylvia. "Marriages Over Half a
Century: A Longitudinal Study." Paper presented at San
Antonio, Texas, by Gerontological Society of America, Nov. 1984.

Fields, Nina S. "Satisfaction in Long-term Marriage." *Social Work,*
Jan.–Feb. 1983, 28, 37–42.

Fliegel, Steffen, Neumann, Helmut, and Paar, Frank. "Communication, Satisfaction and Understanding in Couples: A Model of
Causal Relations and its Empirical Test." *Partnerberating,*
1983, 1, 1–12.

Foote, Nelson N., and Cottrell, Leonard S., Jr. *Identity and
Interpersonal Competence.* Chicago, London: University of
Chicago Press, 1955.

Frank, Ellen, Anderson, Carol and Rubenstein, Debra. "Sexual
Dysfunction in 'Normal' Couples." *New England Journal of
Medicine,* July 20, 1978, 299(3).

Frankel, Charles. "The Impact of Changing Values on the Family."
Social Casework, June 1976, 57,(6), 355–365.

Freud, Sigmund, James Strachey (ed.), *The Standard Edition of the
Complete Psychological Works of Sigmund Freud.* London:
Hogarth Press, Vols. 7, 8, 9, 14, 17, 18, 21, and 22, 1960.

Ginott, Haim G. *Between Parent and Child.* New York: Macmillan,
1965.

Goodman, N., and Ofshe, R. "Empathy, Communication Efficiency
and Marital Status." *Journal of Marriage and the Family.*
Nov., 1968, 30(4), 597–603.

Green, Richard (ed.). *Human Sexuality.* Baltimore, Md.: William and
Wilkins, 1979.

Greenberg, Joel. "Adulthood Comes of Age." *Science News,* July 29,
1978, 114(5), 65–80.

Greenson, Ralph. *Explorations in Psychoanalysis.* New York:
International Universities Press, 1978.

Heiman, Marcel. "The Problems of Family Diagnosis. In Victor W.
Eisenstein, *Neurotic Interaction in Marriage.* New York: Basic
Books, 1956.

Hicks, M. W. and Platt. "Marital Happiness and Stability: A Review
of Research in the Sixties." *Journal of Marriage and the
Family,* 1970, 32(4), 553–574.

Hollingshead, August B. "Cultural Factors in the Selection of
Marriage Mates." *American Sociological Review,* Oct. 1950,
15(5), 619–627.

Hollis, Florence. *Casework, A Psychosocial Therapy.* New York: Random House, 1964.

Jacobson, Edith. *The Self and the Object World.* New York: International Universities Press, 1964.

Jung, C. G. "Marriage as a Psychological Relationsׁהיׂפ" In Herman Keyserling, (ed.), *The Book of Marriage.* New York: Harcourt Brace, 1926, p. 455.

Kaplan, Helen Singer. *The New Sex Therapy.* New York: Brunner/Mazel, 1974.

Kaplan, Helen Singer. *Disorders of Sexual Desire.* New York: Brunner/Mazel, 1979.

Karlsson, Georg. *Adaptability and Communication in Marriage.* Uppsala: Almquist and Wiksells, 1951.

Katchadourian, Herant, and Lunder. *Fundamentals of Human Sexuality.* New York: Holt, Rhinehart & Winston, 1972.

Kernberg, Otto. *Object Relations Theory and Clinical Psychoanalysis.* New York: Jason Aronson, 1976.

Kinsey, Pomeroy, Martin, and Gebhard. *Sexual Behavior in the Human Female.* Philadelphia, London: W. B. Saunders, 1953.

Klein, Melanie. *Love, Guilt and Reparation.* New York: Delacorte Press, 1975.

Kohut, Heinz. *The Analysis of the Self.* New York: International Universities Press, 1971.

Krauss, Ruth. *A Hole is to Dig.* New York: Harper & Row, 1953.

Lederer, William S., and Jackson, Don. *The Mirages of Marriage.* New York: W. W. Norton, 1968.

Levinger, George. "Marital Cohesiveness and Dissolution: An Integrative Review." *Journal of Marriage and the Family,* Feb. 1965, 27(1), 19–28.

Lowenthal, Marjorie Fiske, and Chiriboga, David. "Transition to the Empty Nest: Crisis, Challenge or Relief?" *Archives of General Psychiatry,* Jan. 1972, 26.

Luckey, Eleanore B. "Marital Satisfaction and Its Association with Congruency of Perception." *Journal of Marriage and Family Living,* Feb. 1960, 22(1), 49–54.

Lynn, David B. "The Process of Learning Parental and Sex-Role Identification." *Journal of Marriage and the Family,* Nov. 1966, 28(4), 466–470.

Mahler, Margaret, Pine, Fred, and Bergman, Ann. *The Psychological Birth of the Human Infant: Symbiosis and Individuation.* New York: Basic Books, 1975.

Masters, William H., and Johnson, Virginia E. *Human Sexual Response.* Boston: Little, Brown, 1970.

Maslow, Abraham H. *Toward a Psychology of Being* (2nd ed.). Princeton, N.J.: D. Van Nostrand, 1968.

McKain, W. C. "A New Look at Older Marriages." *Family Coordinator,*

1972, 21(1), 61–70.

Missildine, W. Hugh. *Your Inner Child of the Past.* New York: Simon & Schuster, 1963.

Montagu, Ashley. "Marriage, A Cultural Perspective." In Eisenstein, *Neurotic Interaction in Marriage.* New York: Basic Books, 1956.

Murstein, Bernard I. *Exploring Intimate Life Styles.* New York: Springer, 1978.

Nadelson, C. C., Polansky, D. C., and Mathews, M. A. "Marriage and Midlife: The Impact of Social Change," *Journal of Clinical Psychiatry,* July 1975, 40(7), 242–8.

New York Times. New York: Oct. 10, 1980. "If Your Face Isn't Young: Women Confront Problems of Aging."

O'Neill, Nena, and O'Neill, George. *Open Marriage.* New York: M. Evans, 1972.

Pahl, J. "The Allocation of Money and the Structuring of Inequality Within Marriage." *Sociology Review,* May 1983, 31(2), 237–62.

Perrucci and Targ (eds.). *Marriage and the Family.* New York: David McKay, 1974.

Pfeil, Elisabeth. "Role Expectations When Entering Into Marriage." *Journal of Marriage and the Family,* Feb. 1960, 30(1).

Pickford, John H., Signori, Edro I., and Rempel, Henry. "Similar or Related Personality Traits as a Factor in Marital Happiness." *Journal of Marriage and the Family,* May 1966, 28(2), 190–192.

Pineo, P. C. "Disenchantment in the Late Years of Marriage." *Journal of Marriage and Family Living,*Feb. 1961, 23(1), 3–11.

Polenz, Joanna Magda. *In Defense of Marriage,* New York: Gardner Press, 1981.

Ranasinghe, Alex. "The Betrothal and Marriage Customs of the Hebrews During the Time of Christ." *Folklore* (London:) 18, 1970.

Raush, Harold L., Barry, William A., Hertel, Richard K., and Swain, Mary Ann. *Communication, Conflict and Marriage.* San Francisco: Jossey-Bass, 1974.

Rettig, Kathryn D., and Bubolz, Margaret M. "Interpersonal Resources Exchanges as Indicators of Quality of Marriage." *Journal of Marriage and the Family,* Aug. 1983, 45(3), 497–509.

Rice, David G. *Dual-Career Marriage.* New York: Free Press, 1979.

Rogers, Carl R. *On Becoming a Person.* Boston: Houghton Mifflin, 1961.

Rollins, Boyd, and Feldman, Harold. "Marital Satisfaction Over the Family Life Cycle." *Journal of Marriage and the Family,* Feb. 1970, 32(1), 20–23.

Satir, Virginia. *Conjoint Family Therapy.* Palo Alto, Calif. Science & Behavior Books, 1967.

Schenck, J., Pfrang, H., and Rausche, A. "Personality Traits Versus the Quality of the Marital Relationship as the Determinant of

Marital Sexuality." *Archives of Sexual Behavior,* Feb. 1983, 12(1), 31–42.

Shor, Joel, and Sanville, Jean. *Illusion in Loving.* Los Angeles: Double Helix Press, 1978.

Spanier, G. B. "The Measurement of Marital Quality." *Journal of Sex and Marital Therapy,* Fall 1979, 5(3), 288–300.

Sporakowski, Michael J., and Hughston, George A. "Prescriptions for Happy Marriage: Adjustments and Satisfactions of Couples Married Fifty and More Years." *Family Coordinator,* Oct. 1978, 247(4), 321–327.

Stinnett, Nick, Montgomery, James, and Carter, Linda. "Older Persons Perceptions of Their Marriages." *Journal of Marriage and the Family,* Nov. 1972, 34(4), 655–670.

Stoller, Robert J. *Sexual Excitement.* New York: Pantheon Books, 1979.

Strauss, Anselm. "The Influence of Parent-Images Upon Marital Choice," *American Sociological Review,* Oct. 1946, 10(5), 554–559.

Sussman, Marvin B. *Sourcebook in Marriage and the Family.* Boston: Houghton Mifflin, 1968.

Taylor, Alexander B. "Role Perception, Empathy and Marriage Adjustment."*Sociology and Social Research,* Oct. 1967, 52(22–34.

Terman, Lewis M. *Psychological Factors in Marital Happiness.* New York: McGraw-Hill, 1938.

Terman, Lewis M., and Oden, Melita H. *The Gifted Child Grows Up: Twenty-five Years' Follow-up of a Superior Group.* Stanford: Stanford University Press, 1947.

Tharp, Roland G. "Dimensions of Marriage Roles." *Marriage and Family Living,* Nov. 1963, 25(4), 389–404.

Thornton, A., and Freedman, D. "Changing Attitudes Toward Marriage and Single Life." *Family Planning Perspectives,* Nov./ Dec. 1982, 14(6), 297–303.

Vernon, G. M., and Stewart, R. I. "Empathy as a Process in the Dating Situation." *American Sociological Review,* Feb. 1957, 22(1), 48–52.

Wallin, P. "Marital Happiness of Parents and their Children's Attitude to Marriage." *American Sociological Review,* Feb. 1954. 19(1), 20–23.

Waring, E., McElvath, D., Lefcoe, D., and Weisz, B. "Dimensions of Intimacy in Marriage." *Psychiatry,* May 1981, 44(21), 162–75.

Wexler, Joan and Steidl, John. "Marriage and the Capacity to Be Alone." *Psychiatry,* Feb. 1978, 41.

Wiggins, James D., Wood, Anne D., and Lederer, Doris A. "Personality Typologies Related to Marital Satisfaction." *American Mental Health Counselors Association Journal,* Oct. 1983, 5(4), 169–178.

Winch, Robert F., and Ktsanes, Virginia and Thomas. "The Theory of Complementary Needs in Mate Selection: An Analytic and Descriptive Study." *American Sociological Review*, June 1954, 19(13).

Winch, Robert F., and Goodman, Louis W. *Selected Studies in Marriage and the Family* (3rd ed.), New York: Holt, Rinehart and Winston, 1968.

Index

*A Study of Long-Term
  Successful Marriages,*
  changing times, 13
  children in, 117, 118, 127
  description of, 5
  emotional involvement, 86
  equality, 19
  infidelity, 97
  parents in-law, 155
  parents in need, 157
  separateness-togetherness,
    9, 17
  sexual satisfaction,
    63, 67, 76
Accommodation, 104,105
  as compromise, 105
Anger,
  fear of, 106,107
  rules for, 107, 108
Argumentation, 99
  accomodation, 104, 105
  as communication, 101-104
  avoidance, 112
  conflict-resolution technique,
    108,112
  effective, 100, 102
  ineffective, 110-113
  myths of, 100, 101

Burns, R., 31

Chaucer, G., 25, 109
Canterbury Tales, 25
Celibacy, 163
Children, 117-138
  adolescence, 130-132
  conflict in styles of
    parenting, 125-128
  decision to have, 118, 119
  empty next, 132-136
  living through one's,
    128-130
  power struggles, 128
  stresses, 120-125

Dependency,
  burden of, 17
Divorce,
  effect of children on, 119
  rate of, 3
Down's syndrome, 22

Equality, 15
  for women, 15
Ejaculation, 73
  premature, 71, 73
Empathy, 6, 9, 29
  blocks to, 33-40
  definition, 27, 28
  in argumentation, 108
  in having children, 119
Expectations,
  trouble with, 21-25

Fantasy, 21, 22, 94
  fears and, 34, 35
Fear,
  and fantasies, 34, 35
  of anger, 106-109
  of differences, 36
Feminism, 3, 14
Freud, S., 37, 143
Friendship,
  with mate, 10, 11
  with others, 11, 12

Incompleteness,
  myth of, 16, 17
Independence, 19, 26
Infidelity, 81-97
  deceit, 89
In-laws,
  building relations with,
    154-156
Interests,
  separate, 12, 13

League of Woman Voters, 19
Lying, 89-91

Marriage,
  and infidelity, 81-97
  author's definition of, 164
  celibacy in, 163
  child-rearing in, 117-138
  communication in, 105, 106
  divorce rate, 3
  empty nest, 132-136
  egalitarian, 21
  "failed", 4
  gay, 163
  in media, 3
  long-term, 4-6
  midlife, impact on, 95-97
  money in, 43-59
  parental influence on, 139-159
  relations with in-laws, 154-156
  sexual intercourse in, frequency, 62, 63
  sexual satisfaction in, 63, 64
  "successful", 4
  troubled, 4
  trust in, 64-67
Masturbation, 70
Midlife,
  impact on marriage, 95-97
Money, 43-59
  as control, 54-57
  as reward, 53
  in second marriages, 51-53
  language of, 44-48
Monogamy,
  "burden of", 82-84

Oedipus complex, 37,38
Open Marriage, 85
Oral sex, 66
Orgasm, 65, 67, 72

Parents,
  as models, 143-148
  caring for, 156-159
  impossible standards, 149-151
  influence of, 139-159
  in mate selection, 140-143
  meddling, 151
  relations with in-laws, 154-156
  separation from, 148, 149
  unexamined images, 36-39
Parent Teacher Association (PTA), 19, 95
Preconceptions, 39, 40
Psychotherapy,
  4, 33, 38, 92, 106, 119
  "crisis therapy", 132

Self knowledge, 30, 31, 33
  sense of self, 31, 32
Separateness-togetherness, 13, 16, 17, 23
Separation,
  as distinct from divorce, 94, 151
  from parents, 148, 149
Sex models,
  imperfect adult, 36-39
Sexuality, 61-80
  affection, 75
  and emotions, 85-88
  making changes, 75, 76
  sexual intercourse frequency in marriage, 62, 63
  specifics, 71, 72
  "switching", 93
  trust, 64-67
Sexual satisfaction, 6
  openness, 67-76
  trust, 64-67
  what is, 63, 64
Stress, 91, 92
"Switching", 93, 98

The Cinderella Complex, 16
Trust, 64-67, 84, 89, 97

Women's movement, 87
Work, 19
  and independence, 19-21